# SOUTH CAROLINA PATRIOTS

## Their Lives, Contributions, and Burial Sites

JOE FARRELL • LAWRENCE KNORR • JOE FARLEY

Mechanicsburg, PA USA

Published by Sunbury Press, Inc.
Mechanicsburg, Pennsylvania

www.sunburypress.com

Copyright © 2025 by Joe Farrell, Joe Farley, and Lawrence Knorr.
Cover Copyright © 2025 by Sunbury Press, Inc.

Sunbury Press supports copyright. Copyright fuels creativity, encourages diverse voices, promotes free speech, and creates a vibrant culture. Thank you for buying an authorized edition of this book and for complying with copyright laws by not reproducing, scanning, or distributing any part of it in any form without permission. You are supporting writers and allowing Sunbury Press to continue to publish books for every reader. For information contact Sunbury Press, Inc., Subsidiary Rights Dept., PO Box 548, Boiling Springs, PA 17007 USA or legal@sunburypress.com.

For information about special discounts for bulk purchases, please contact Sunbury Press Orders Dept. at (855) 338-8359 or orders@sunburypress.com.

To request one of our authors for speaking engagements or book signings, please contact Sunbury Press Publicity Dept. at publicity@sunburypress.com.

FIRST SUNBURY PRESS EDITION: September 2025

Set in Adobe Garamond | Interior design by Crystal Devine | Cover by Lawrence Knorr | Edited by the authors.

Publisher's Cataloging-in-Publication Data
Names: Farrell, Joe, author | Farley, Joe, author | Knorr, Lawrence, author.
Title: South Carolina patriots : their lives, contributions, and burial sites / Joe Farrell Lawrence Knorr Joe Farley.
Description: First trade paperback edition. | Mechanicsburg, PA : Sunbury Press, 2025.
Summary: The individuals from South Carolina who played prominent roles in the founding of the USA are detailed.
Identifiers: ISBN 979-8-88819-389-1 (softcover).
Subjects: HISTORY / United States / Revolutionary Period (1775-1800) | BIOGRAPHY & AUTOBIOGRAPHY / Political.

Designed in the USA
0 1 1 2 3 5 8 13 21 34 55

*For the Love of Books!*

# Contents

Introduction ............................................... v

**Henry Laurens** First President of the Recognized USA.................. 1
**William Richardson Davie** Hero of Stone Ferry.................. 8
**Johann Robais, Baron de Kalb** French Major General ............ 13
**Christopher Gadsden** "Sam Adams of the South"................... 17
**Thomas Heyward Jr.** The Last to Sign the Declaration................. 23
**Richard Hutson** First Mayor of Charleston...................... 29
**Francis Marion** Swamp Fox................................ 34
**John Mathews** "The Disagreeable One" ........................ 43
**Arthur Middleton** Defender of Charleston...................... 48
**Henry Middleton** "The Interim President" ...................... 54
**William Moultrie** Hero of Sullivan's Island...................... 59
**Andrew Pickens** The Wizard Owl ............................ 64
**Charles Pinckney** Proponent of Slavery........................ 69
**Charles Cotesworth Pinckney** XYZ Affair .................... 74
**Edward Rutledge** Youngest to Sign the Declaration .................. 81
**John Rutledge** "The Dictator"............................... 86
**Thomas Sumter** Carolina Gamecock.......................... 93

Sources................................................. 100
Index .................................................. 104

# Introduction

Most people who know anything about the American Revolution would assume either Philadelphia or Boston would be the location of the most Founders' graves. After all, Philadelphia was the center of government for most of the period, and Boston was where much of the early action took place. A more astute scholar would point out the importance of New York City as a place where great battles were fought and where a significant amount of trade was conducted. It was also the nation's capital for several years of the Early Republic. Few would guess Charleston, South Carolina, has more Founders' graves than Boston! Yes, the Palmetto State was prominent during the Revolution and is often overlooked, perhaps due to its subsequent history in the Civil War. Only Philadelphia (26) and New York (14) surpass Charleston (13). (Boston has 11.)

Besides the agitators and thought leaders, South Carolina was also the home of several great military leaders who were tested in important and decisive battles. The Southern Theater of the American Revolution was a highly active region, characterized by intense conflict between Loyalists and Patriots and unconventional tactics. As the tide was turned, victories in the South were precursors to the British surrender at Yorktown. Let's not forget that following the disastrous Siege of Charleston and the loss at Camden, there were important victories at Kings Mountain and Cowpens.

South Carolinian Henry Laurens leads off this volume. Although a largely forgotten figure in American history, Laurens was very important at the time, especially during his tenure as President of the Continental Congress from November 1, 1777, to December 9, 1778. He was nominated for the position during the darkest hours of the Revolution, after the Congress had fled Philadelphia just before the British captured it. While in exile in York, Pennsylvania, then-President John Hancock decided he was better off back in Boston and resigned. Laurens filled the vacancy and quipped, "At least I will sit closer to the woodstove!" Laurens then led the nation through the victory at Saratoga, the failed Conway Cabal, the Treaty of Alliance with France, and the creation of our first constitution, the Articles of Confederation. Yes, Laurens led the nation through the turning point of the Revolution, at a time when the new nation was recognized abroad and established its government.

Key among the Patriots of South Carolina were the wealthy planters, including the Pinckneys, Rutledges, and Middletons. Among them were Presidents of Congress, governors, and future presidential candidates.

Christopher Gadsden was a prominent agitator, often referred to as the "Sam Adams of the South." Other great men of Charleston who played prominent roles were Mayor Richard Hutson, irascible John Mathews, and Thomas Heyward Jr., the last to sign the Declaration of Independence.

But it is the generals who carry the day. William Moultrie successfully defended Sullivan's Island in 1776 by using the trunks of palmetto trees to deter British cannonballs, leading to the use of the palmetto on the current state flag. William Richardson Davie led at Stone Ferry. Johan Robais, Baron de Kalb, gave his life at Camden. Francis Marion deceived the British with his tactics, earning the moniker "Swamp Fox." Thomas Sumter and Andrew Pickens were also fierce fighters, the latter one of the heroes at Cowpens.

Please enjoy the retelling of our founding through the brief biographies of these citizens of South Carolina. Always remember: "Poor is the nation that has no heroes, but poorer still is the nation that having heroes, fails to remember and honor them." (attributed to Marcus Tullius Cicero)

Lawrence Knorr, Ph.D.
September 2025

# Henry Laurens
## (1724–1792)

### First President of the Recognized USA

Buried at Laurens Family Cemetery,
Moncks Corner, Berkeley County, South Carolina.

**Articles of Confederation**

Henry Laurens was a South Carolina plantation owner, merchant, and partner in the largest slave-trading house in North America. Laurens was active in state and national politics as the Vice President of South Carolina, Continental Congressman, and President of Congress. He signed the Articles of Confederation, presiding over its adoption. He was also the Minister to the Hague during the Revolution but was captured by the British on his return and imprisoned in the Tower of London for fifteen months.

Laurens, born on March 6, 1724, in Charleston, South Carolina, was the eldest son and third child of Jean Samuel Laurens and Hester (née Grasset) Laurens. His father was of French Huguenot descent, arriving with his parents in New York in the late 1600s. About 1715 or 1716, the elder Laurens married a French Huguenot wife from Staten Island; the young couple moved to Charleston, South Carolina, where Henry was born a decade later. Mother Hester Laurens died in 1741, and her husband remarried Elizabeth Wickling. Jean Samuel Laurens then passed in 1747, leaving his estate to his eldest son, Henry.

# SOUTH CAROLINA PATRIOTS

Henry Laurens

Laurens was initially educated in Charleston. In 1744, at age 19, he went to England to study business with Richard Oswald, the principal owner of Bunce Island, a slave-trading island base in the Sierra Leone River of Africa. He stayed there until his father's death three years later.

Leveraging his inheritance, Laurens quickly rose as a leader of the merchant class in Charleston, trading with England and the West Indies. His plantation on the Cooper River employed over 300 slaves, and he was an active importer and trader of slaves throughout the colonies.

On June 25, 1750, Laurens married Eleanor Ball, the daughter of a South Carolina rice planter. The couple had thirteen children, most of them dying in childhood. During the 1750s, Laurens held local offices and, in 1757, was elected to the Commons House of Assembly, staying there through the beginning of the Revolution in 1775, except for 1773, when he arranged his sons' education in England.

From 1757 to 1761, Laurens was also a lieutenant colonel in the militia, fighting a campaign against the Cherokee during the French and

## Henry Laurens (1724–1792)

Indian War. During the spring of 1760, smallpox raged throughout the low country of South Carolina. Lauren's infant daughter, Martha, apparently succumbed to the disease. As was customary, her little body was laid on a bed by an open window. The family then gathered around for a wake for the deceased. Outside, a light rain began to fall, and a cool breeze blew a few droplets on the young girl's head. She began to stir, clearly not dead. The child had narrowly avoided being buried alive! Little Martha recovered, married Dr. David Ramsay, and lived a full life.

In 1764 and 1768, Laurens was named to the King's Council of South Carolina but declined. Wife Eleanor died in 1770 of complications from the childbirth of their last child. Laurens left his local offices to care for his children and then, realizing the harsh impacts of British trade policies, traveled to London to attempt to unsuccessfully negotiate a resolution.

In 1772, Laurens joined the American Philosophical Society of Philadelphia and became well-acquainted with the other members. In 1773, on the eve of the Revolution, Laurens took his three sons to England to be educated. John, the oldest, studied law. However, he returned to America in 1776 and served in the Revolution.

Meanwhile, in South Carolina, Laurens, who initially hoped for reconciliation with England, was elected to the Provincial Congress on January 9, 1775. As he became convinced of the need for independence, he became the President of the Committee of Safety and presided over the Congress from June until March 1776. He was then appointed the Vice President of South Carolina through June 27, 1777.

Laurens was elected to the Continental Congress on January 10, 1777, serving until 1780. From November 1, 1777, until December 9, 1778, he was the President of Congress, succeeding John Hancock. During this time, he oversaw the debate and creation of the Articles of Confederation while the Congress was in York, Pennsylvania. Laurens signed the document as President. He then led the transfer of the Congress back to Philadelphia on July 2, 1778.

Congress named Laurens the Minister to the Hague (Netherlands) in the fall of 1779. In early 1780, he traveled to Amsterdam and gained Dutch support for the colonies. However, on his return trip, while aboard the packet *Mercury* off the coast of Newfoundland, Laurens was captured by the HMS *Vestal*. Laurens tossed his dispatches in the water, but they were recovered. Among them was the draft of a treaty with the Dutch that prompted the British to declare war on the Dutch Republic, triggering the Fourth Anglo-Dutch War. Laurens, charged with treason, was examined by British officials. Some of the interrogation by Lord Hillsborough was published in newspapers in England and the colonies:

> "Is your name Henry Laurens?"
>
> "It is."
>
> "Are you the same Henry Laurens who was the President of the Congress in America?"
>
> "I am."
>
> "We are ordered by the King and Council to examine you and have certain questions to propose."
>
> "Your Lordships may save yourselves the trouble of an examination, as I think it my place to answer no questions you may put."
>
> "Sir, we are directed to commit you [as a] prisoner to the Tower."
>
> "I am ready to attend."

Thus, former President Henry Laurens became the only American held prisoner in the Tower of London. Fortunately, his former business mentor, Richard Oswald, still thought fondly of him and lobbied for his release. This finally occurred on December 31, 1781, when he was exchanged for General Lord Cornwallis, who was captured at Yorktown. He came home to find his plantation home, Mepkin, had been burned by the British, and the family lived in an outbuilding while they recovered.

Tragically, Colonel John Laurens, Henry's eldest son, was killed in 1782 at the Battle of the Combahee River before the Treaty of Paris ended the war. Father and son had argued over the years about the evils of slavery. John had urged his father to free his slaves and had offered the 40 he was to inherit to the cause, but Laurens did not relent and never manumitted his slaves.

In 1783, Laurens was sent to Paris to assist in negotiating peace with Britain, whose principal negotiator was Richard Oswald. Laurens, though not a signer of the Treaty of Paris, helped to negotiate settlements for the Netherlands and Spain.

Following the Revolution, Laurens retired from public life, declining to continue service in the Continental Congress or the Constitutional Convention. However, he served briefly in the state convention in South Carolina in 1788 for the ratification of the US Constitution.

Laurens died from complications of gout on December 8, 1792, at Mepkin. Due to his fear of being accidentally buried alive, the family waited three days before proceeding with his funeral. Laurens' will ordered the following:

> I come to the disposal of my own person. I solemnly enjoin it on my son (Henry Jr.) as an indispensable duty, that as soon as he conveniently can after my decease, he cause my Body to be wrapped in twelve yards of tow cloth, and burnt until it be entirely and totally consumed. And then collecting my bones, deposit them where ever he shall think proper.

Laurens is believed to be the first Caucasian to be cremated in the United States. However, it did not go well. The pyre was built along the banks of the Cooper River, and his remains were burned as wished. Accounts vary, but due to the amount of fluid in the body, the liquid poured forth and extinguished most of the flames prematurely. Then, the head broke from the corpse, hair aflame, and rolled down the bank into reeds by the water. A slave was sent into the mud to perform the gruesome task of retrieving it. His remaining bones, ashes, and charred head were then buried in the family plot at Moncks Corner, now on the grounds of Mepkin Abbey.

Some in the press did not approve of Laurens' method of disposal. There was a sonnet by someone using the penname Amicus titled "Lines written on reading the singular manner in which Henry Laurens, Esq. ordered his corpse to be disposed of." It read:

> The Pagans oft their funeral piles have made,
> To offer victims, or consume their dead;

> But who in Christian lands, e'er built a fire
> To expatiate their crimes, or burn a Sire!
> Will Christian people dread the worms of earth,
> Since they expect to rise to second birth?
> When Jesus bids the grave its prey resign,
> In his blest likeness they may hope to shine.

The city and county of Laurens, South Carolina, are named for Laurens. The village of Laurens in New York is also named for him. Laurens County, Georgia, is named for his son John. Fort Laurens in Ohio was named for Henry by his friend, General Lachlan McIntosh. Historian C. James Taylor summarized Laurens as follows:

> In both his public and private life, Henry Laurens' commitment to duty and hard work were recognized and admired. Unfortunately, his impatience and criticism of individuals who did not meet his

The gravestone of Henry Laurens, who was cremated.

standards made him appear petty and inflexible. As the strongest political figure in South Carolina during the transition from provincial to state government, he worked to protect the rights of Loyalists and moderate the zeal of the radicals. In Congress, his constancy during the British occupation of Philadelphia and the trying exile at York may have been his most significant contribution to the national cause. The poor health he endured after confinement in the tower and the emotional shock of his son John's death in August 1782 robbed him of the vigor that had marked his career to that time.

Warning of the dangers near the grave of Henry Laurens.

# William Richardson Davie
## (1756–1820)

### Hero of Stone Ferry

Buried at Old Waxhaw Presbyterian Church Cemetery,
Lancaster, South Carolina.

---

**Military**

Born in England, this Founder served honorably fighting against the British during the Revolutionary War. Even after suffering a serious wound and barely escaping capture, he chose to return to the field of battle after he recovered. After the war, he was elected to the North Carolina House of Commons multiple times. He served as a member of his state's delegation to the 1787 Constitutional Convention. Though he strongly supported the product produced by that gathering, he was not present for the signing ceremony. He argued vigorously for its ratification at the North Carolina state conventions held in 1788 and 1789. He served as governor of North Carolina and as a diplomat on a 1799 peace commission in France. He is considered the Founder of the University of North Carolina. His name was William Richardson Davie.

Davie was born on June 20, 1756, in the village of Egremont, England. His father brought him to the American colonies in 1763. His uncle on his mother's side, the Reverend William Richardson after whom he was named, adopted his nephew and made him his son and heir. When Richardson passed away, Davie inherited 150 acres and a large library. From this point on, he always used his full name as a way to honor his uncle. He was educated locally before attending what is

## William Richardson Davie (1756–1820)

Posthumous portrait of William Richardson Davie, painted by Charles Willson Peale in 1826.

now Princeton University. Among his fellow students at the time were Jonathon Dayton, Gunning Bedford, Jr., and James Madison. If the phrase 'we're getting the band back together' had been in vogue at the time this quartet could have used it prior to the 1787 Constitutional Convention.

After leaving Princeton, Davie applied himself to the study of law until this effort was interrupted by the Revolution. In 1778, he decided to join a militia force commanded by General Allen Jones. Jones directed his force to Charleston, South Carolina with the intention of providing for the defense of the port city against a British attack. When the English threat failed to materialize, the troops returned to North Carolina.

In 1779, Davie raised and trained a cavalry troop. The troop was assigned to serve under General Casimir Pulaski who promoted Davie to the rank of major. On June 20, 1779, Davie led a charge against the British forces during the Battle of Stone Ferry. It was during this engagement that his thigh was seriously wounded and he was thrown from his horse. Fortunate to avoid capture, he spent five months in a Charleston hospital recovering from his injuries.

By 1780 Davie had regained his health and once again formed a company of cavalry. He was ordered to protect the region between Charlotte and Camden and performed the duties so well that he was made colonel commandant of the cavalry of North Carolina.

During this time the British led by General Cornwallis had begun an invasion of the southern states. When the invaders under the command of Colonel Tarleton entered Charlotte, Davie twice led aggressive assaults on the enemy forces despite being heavily outnumbered. When the English forces retreated two weeks later, Davie ordered his men to disrupt their withdrawal through skirmishes with the enemy units.

On August 16, 1780, American forces under the command of General Horatio Gates were soundly defeated in the Battle of Camden. Gates rallied his defeated forces and retreated into North Carolina. Davie didn't move his forces north with Gates. Instead he headed south towards the enemy with the goal of recovering abandoned supply wagons and gathering information on the movement of the British forces. So successful was this endeavor that it cost Davie his field command. General Gates was in desperate need of more provisions and so impressed with Davie that he was appointed to the post of commissary-general. In this position, he oversaw the locating, organizing, and transportation of supplies for the troops under Gates' command.

After the revolution, Davie's prominence in North Carolina grew as both a lawyer and a public speaker. He became involved politically and was elected to the North Carolina House of Commons. In 1787, he was sent to Philadelphia as one of North Carolina's representatives at the Constitutional Convention.

Davie was much involved in resolving one of the major issues facing those at the convention. That question involved the delicate issue of slavery and how the slaves, held largely in the south, would be counted in determining representation in the House of Representatives. Many

## William Richardson Davie (1756–1820)

of the northern delegates objected to the slaves being counted at all. A compromise that would have counted each slave as three-fifths of a free citizen was rejected on July 11th by a vote of six states to four. Every northern state except Connecticut voted against the proposal. South Carolina remained opposed to the compromise as their delegates were insisting that every slave be counted the same as a free person. After the vote, Davie drew a line in the sand saying that North Carolina "would never confederate on any terms that did not rate them [slaves} at least as three-fifths," he then went on to declare that if the south were denied a share of representation for their black slaves then the work of the convention "was at an end."

Davie was among the delegates chosen to serve on a committee to propose a solution to the stalemate. The result was the "Great Compromise." The proposal that resulted was that the three-fifths rule would apply both in apportioning direct taxes and in determining representation in the House. The northern states were attracted to the additional tax revenues and the southern states satisfied by the partial counting of their slaves. The proposal was approved unanimously. In his 1966 book titled *1787: The Grand Convention*, Clinton Rossiter described Davie as "an agent if not an architect of the Great Compromise."

Davie returned to North Carolina before the Constitution was signed but he was a strong advocate for ratification at his state conventions in

The grave of William Richardson Davie at Old Waxhaw Presbyterian Church Cemetery in Riverside, South Carolina (photo by Lawrence Knorr).

both 1788 and 1789. He voiced his frustration with those who opposed ratification saying, "It is much easier to alarm people than to inform them."

In 1798, Davie was elected Governor of North Carolina. He resigned the office a year later when President Adams requested that he serve on a peace commission to France. A staunch Federalist, Davie made an unsuccessful run for a seat in the House of Representatives in 1804. During the war of 1812, he served in the army but declined an offer to be appointed Major General from President Madison. Davie died at his estate in South Carolina on November 29, 1820. He was laid to rest in the Old Waxhaw Presbyterian Church Cemetery.

Davie earned acclaim as a soldier, a politician, and a diplomat but his accomplishments didn't end there. As a member of the North Carolina legislature, he sponsored a bill that chartered the University of North Carolina. He laid the cornerstone of the university in October of 1793 and is recognized as the founder of the institution.

# Johann Robais, Baron de Kalb
## (1721 – 1780)

### French Major General

Buried at Bethesda Presbyterian Churchyard,
Camden, South Carolina.

**Military**

Born in what is now Germany, Major General Johann de Kalb served with honor in the Continental Army during the American Revolutionary War. After arriving in America with the Marquis de Lafayette, de Kalb played a key role in shaping the early U.S. Army—training and leading Soldiers, instilling discipline, and strengthening the force during its formative years. He led troops through the harsh winter at Valley Forge and later commanded forces in the Southern Campaign. At the Battle of Camden in 1780, de Kalb was mortally wounded while leading troops from Maryland and Delaware in fierce combat. His final words reflected the heart of a true patriot: "I die the death I always prayed for—the death of a soldier fighting for the rights of man."

De Kalb was born in Hüttendorf, a German village near Erlangen, Principality of Bayreuth, on June 29, 1721, the son of Johann Kalb and Margarethe Seitz. He went to school at Kriegenbronn and left home when he was sixteen. He received his first military training in 1743 as a Lieutenant in a German regiment of the French infantry. He served with distinction in the War of the Austrian Succession and in the Seven Years'

Johan de Kalb

War. He was promoted to Lt. Colonel and made Assistant Quartermaster General in the Army of the Upper Rhine. In 1763, he was awarded the Order of Military Merit and elevated to the nobility with the title of Baron.

In 1764, de Kalb resigned from the Army, got married, and started farming near Versailles. His wife was Anna Elizabeth Emilie Van Robais, a French heiress. The couple had three children.

In 1768, he was sent to the colonies as a secret agent to determine the sentiment of the colonists towards the British. He traveled extensively throughout the colonies, clandestinely observing the temperament of the colonists. He was arrested on suspicion of spying but was released for lack of evidence. When he returned to Paris, his report to the French government told of the dissatisfaction of the colonies with British rule.

In July 1777, de Kalb returned to America with his protégé, the Marquis de Lafayette, and joined the Continental Army. He had

## Johann Robais, Baron de Kalb (1721–1780)

previously met with Benjamin Franklin and an American diplomat named Silas Deane in Paris to discuss joining the Continental Army, and Deane, citing the Continental Army's need for experienced officers, promised de Kalb a major general's commission. He was disappointed and angry to learn that he would not be made a Major General and arranged for his return to France. He was, however, appointed to the rank on September 5, 1777, due to Lafayette's influence.

De Kalb was with George Washington's army during the winter at Valley Forge, the Monmouth Campaign, and the operations around New York City.

In the fall of 1779, the British commander Sir Henry Clinton decided to focus on the Southern colonies. Clinton's first target was Charleston. Major General Benjamin Lincoln and 5,000 Americans defended Charleston. Clinton opened the siege in April 1780. Washington, hoping to reinforce Lincoln's garrison, sent de Kalb to South Carolina. De Kalb and his men were unable to reach Lincoln in time. Lincoln surrendered to Clinton on May 12, 1780.

In response to the fall of Charleston, Congress appointed Major General Horatio Gates to lead the American Army in the South. Gates decided to strike the British, now led by Lord Charles Cornwallis, at one of the British outposts at Camden, South Carolina. On August 16, the two armies clashed. It quickly went badly for the Americans. The Virginia and North Carolina militias broke ranks and fled before a vicious bayonet charge. The American panic got even worse when Cornwallis ordered a cavalry unit to move in on the rear of the American forces. De Kalb attempted to rally his troops during the confusion, but de Kalb's horse was shot from under him, causing him to tumble to the ground. Before he could get up, he was shot three times and bayonetted repeatedly by British soldiers.

It is reported that Cornwallis supervised the dressing of de Kalb's wounds by his own surgeons. It was then that de Kalb issued his last words as previously reported. He died three days later, August 19, 1780, at the age of fifty-nine. He was buried near the hospital where he died. In 1825, he was disinterred and reburied beneath a monument in the yard of the Bethesda Presbyterian Church on East DeKalb Street in Camden.

Death of de Kalb at Camden.

His original headstone is now part of the foundation of the steps of the Kershaw County Chamber of Commerce.

Upon visiting de Kalb's grave several years after his death, George Washington is reported to have said: "So there lies the brave de Kalb. The generous stranger, who came from a distant land to fight our battles and to water with his blood the tree of liberty. Would to God he had lived to share its fruits."

Grave of Johann de Kalb

# Christopher Gadsden
## (1724 – 1805)

### "Sam Adams of the South"

Buried at St. Philip's Churchyard,
Charleston, South Carolina.

**Continental Association • Brigadier General**

Christopher Gadsden was a Charleston merchant, brigadier general in the South Carolina state militia, lieutenant governor of South Carolina, and Continental Congressman who signed the Continental Association. He designed a flag with a coiled rattlesnake waiting to strike in defense while sitting on a tuft of grass, a yellow field behind it. The flag became known as the Gadsden Flag.

Gadsden was born on February 16, 1724, in Charleston, South Carolina, to Thomas Gadsden and his wife, Elizabeth Gadsden. The elder Gadsden was the customs collector for the Port of Charleston after being a lieutenant in the Royal Navy. The grandfather, Edward Gadsden, had emigrated to South Carolina from England in 1695. Christopher was the only child from Thomas's first marriage to survive to adulthood. Gadsden's mother died when he was a boy. As a teenager, Gadsden was sent to live with relatives in England to attend school and learn the classics.

Gadsden's father died in 1741 when Christopher was only seventeen. In 1741, he was back in America, serving as an apprentice at a

Christopher Gadsden

Philadelphia counting-house, when his father passed. At that time, he inherited a large fortune. As a young man, he was also the purser on the British warship HMS *Aldborough* from 1745 to 1746 during King George's War.

Later, in 1746, Gadsden married Jane Godfrey. By 1747, he had compiled enough capital to repurchase lands sold by his father under duress. In 1750, he built Beneventum Plantation House near Georgetown, South Carolina. Gadsden and his wife had one child, a daughter, Elizabeth.

In 1757, Gadsden was elected to the Commons House of Assembly in South Carolina. He was also the captain of a militia company that fought against the Cherokee in 1759. However, tragedy struck that year when his wife, Jane, died at only 29, leaving Christopher with young Elizabeth.

By 1761, Gadsden was well-known as a prosperous merchant and plantation owner in the Charleston area. He dealt in fine goods, indigo, furs, and rice. He added ships to his holdings and began selling slaves. He became known as a "Country Factor," someone who dealt with the local produce, as opposed to a merchant who traded with England. He next married Mary Hasell, with whom he had a daughter and a son.

In 1762, Governor Boone, out of concern for voting irregularities, dissolved the Commons. Gadsden's reelection was one that was questioned as he earned eighty percent of the vote in a three-way race. When the governor held the elections again, Gadsden still won, leading to tension with the royal government that would last for years.

Gadsden reacted harshly to the Sugar Act (1764) and Stamp Act (1765) and was selected to represent South Carolina at the Stamp Act Congress in New York City. He refused to participate in any conciliatory discussions, instead arguing for the colonists' rights. This came to Samuel Adams' attention, and the two began a long friendship. Gadsden was eventually known as the "Sam Adams of the South." After the Stamp Act was repealed, Gadsden was one of three South Carolinians, including Thomas Lynch and John Rutledge, who had their portraits painted at state expense. Thus, he was one of the founding members of the Sons of Liberty in South Carolina.

In 1767, Gadsden completed the wharf in Charleston Harbor that bears his name. Between its erection and 1808, it is believed that nearly 40% of all enslaved Africans who entered the colonies were processed through this wharf.

Tragedy struck the Gadsden house again in 1769 when his wife, Mary, passed away, leaving two young children. Gadsden, now in his mid-forties, married once more, Anne Wragg, with whom he stayed the rest of his life.

As hostilities increased with England, Gadsden rose to the rank of lieutenant colonel in the militia. He was also elected as a delegate to the First Continental Congress in 1774 along with Thomas Heyward, Jr., Thomas Lynch, Henry Middleton, and Edward Rutledge. John Adams recorded some observations about Gadsden:

> Visited Mr. Gadsden, Mr. Deane, Colonel Dyer, etc. at their lodgings. Gadsden is violent against allowing to Parliament any power of regulating trade, or allowing that they have anything to do with

us. 'Power of regulating trade,' he says, 'is power of ruining us; as bad as acknowledging them a supreme legislative in all cases whatsoever; a right of regulating trade is a right of legislation, and a right of legislation in one case is a right in all; this I deny.' Attended the Congress and committee all the forenoon . . .

Silas Deane observed about Gadsden:

(Christopher Gadsden) leaves all New England Sons of Liberty far behind, for he is for taking up his firelock and marching direct to Boston; nay, he affirmed this morning, that were his wife and all his children in Boston, and they were to perish by the sword, it would not alter his sentiment or proceeding for American liberty.

Despite the harm that it did to his trade business, Gadsden signed the Continental Association, boycotting trade with England.

Gadsden was elected to the Second Continental Congress in 1775 and assigned to the Marine Committee, outfitting the country's first naval mission under the direction of George Washington. At the time, the Marines carried drums painted yellow depicting a coiled rattlesnake with thirteen rattles and the motto "Don't Tread on Me." Realizing the new US Navy needed a flag, Gadsden borrowed the design from the drums and utilized it for a yellow rattlesnake flag he gave to Commodore Esek Hopkins, who used it as his personal standard on his flagship, the USS *Alfred* on December 20, 1775 while the ship was near Philadelphia.

On February 9, 1776, before returning to South Carolina to command the 1st South Carolina Regiment of the Continental Army and aid in the defense of Charleston, Gadsden gave President of Congress William Henry Drayton an example of the flag. This flag has since become known as the Gadsden Flag.

Back in South Carolina, in addition to his military duties, Gadsden served in the state house. In 1778, Gadsden participated in the convention to draft a new constitution for South Carolina. He was then named the lieutenant governor of the state, replacing Henry Laurens, who was off to the Continental Congress.

### Christopher Gadsden (1724–1805)

When Charleston fell to the British in 1780, Governor John Rutledge fled the state to North Carolina to be a "government in exile." Meanwhile Gadsden stayed behind and surrendered the city. He was paroled at his house in Charleston. However, when General Cornwallis took over for General Clinton, the British were harsher towards the parolees and sent twenty men, including Gadsden, to the old Spanish fortress, Castillo de San Marcos, in St. Augustine, Florida. There, he stayed for forty-two weeks.

Grave of Christopher Gadsden

When released in 1781, Gadsden learned of the British defeat at Cowpens and Cornwallis's movement towards Yorktown. He returned to South Carolina to restore the government.

Though elected governor in 1782, Gadsden declined on his health, having suffered in the prison in Florida. Instead, John Mathews became governor. Gadsden remained involved in the state house, however, and was against the confiscation of the property of Loyalists who had fled the state. In 1788, Gadsden was a member of the state convention to ratify the new US Constitution. During the intervening years, Gadsden was a strong supporter of both Presidents Washington and Adams.

Gadsden built a house at 329 East Bay Street in Charleston in 1798. It incorporated the snake motif from the Gadsden flag in the iron works.

Following an accidental fall on August 28, 1805, Gadsden died in Charleston. He was buried in St. Philip's Churchyard in the city alongside his parents. Charleston's *City Gazette* reported at the time:

> The long and meritorious services of this most valuable and lamented citizen are too well known to his countrymen to require a lengthy recital of them here—suffice it to say, that he was one of the earliest patriots of Carolina and the revolution; that as a soldier in the field, as a statesman of our councils, and in the private walks of the citizen, his whole life was devoted to the service of his country.

The Gadsden Purchase of Arizona was named for Gadsden's grandson, James. Battery Gadsden on Sullivan's Island at Fort Moultrie is named after him.

# Thomas Heyward Jr.
## (1746–1809)

### The Last to Sign the Declaration

Buried at Heyward Family Cemetery,
Old House, South Carolina.

---

**Declaration of Independence • Articles of Confederation • Military**

Thomas Heyward Jr. was a wealthy planter from South Carolina who, as a Continental Congressman, signed the Declaration of Independence and the Articles of Confederation. He also fought in the South Carolina militia during the Siege of Charleston.

---

Heyward was born on July 28, 1746, at the family estate "Old House," near Beaufort, Jasper County, South Carolina, the son of Daniel Heyward and his wife, Mary (née Miles) Heyward. Oddly, the family already had a son named Thomas when Heyward was born, and they liked the name so much that they had another and appended "Junior" to it. The Heyward ancestors were among the first to settle in what was then Carolina in 1670 and became wealthy planters.

In his early years, Heyward was educated at home. Then he decided to study law and traveled to London to attend the Middle Temple, starting on January 10, 1765. He achieved the bar on May 25, 1770.

The following year, now twenty-five, Heyward returned to South Carolina and was admitted to the bar there. He then followed in his father's footsteps as a planter and attorney. Next, the young scion found

Thomas Heyward Jr.

himself elected to the South Carolina Commons House of Assembly in 1772, where he served for several years.

When tensions rose with England, Heyward was a delegate to the South Carolina provincial convention to determine the course of action in the colony. During this time, Heyward married Elizabeth Matthews of Charleston, the sister of John Mathews, a future governor of South Carolina. The couple had two sons.

When the new General Assembly was formed, Heyward was elected to it and appointed to the Council of Safety, serving in 1775 and 1776. On February 16, 1776, the General Assembly elected Heyward to a seat in the Continental Congress. He attended sessions from April 24, 1776, to September 4, 1776. During this time, he signed the Declaration of Independence and was likely the last to do so.

Heyward then returned to South Carolina and served in the General Assembly again. He was reelected to the Continental Congress and served from December 24, 1776, until October 31, 1777. During this time, he escaped with the Congress to York, Pennsylvania, and signed the Articles of Confederation.

Again, Heyward headed home to South Carolina, alternating between his plantation "White Hall" and his home in Charleston. In 1778, Heyward became a judge. At one trial, Heyward presided over a treason trial for several traitors. They were convicted and executed within sight of the British.

When the British besieged Charleston, Heyward took up arms, fighting with General William Moultrie. He was badly wounded and unable to escape when the British took the city. On August 27, 1780, he was captured, and all 130 of his slaves were taken as booty, and then White Hall was burned. For this loss, he was later described by the press as a "martyr of the revolution."

Heyward and 28 others were taken to a ship in Charleston harbor. On September 4, they were moved to St. Augustine, Florida, where they remained until they were exchanged eleven months later. To pass the time in prison, Heyward rewrote the British song "God Save the King" and to reflect an American version, changing the title to "God Save the Thirteen States."

During his captivity, his wife and children lived in Philadelphia. Unfortunately, while awaiting his release, she died in childbirth in 1782. She was buried in the St. Peter's Episcopal Churchyard in Philadelphia. Although they had six children, only Daniel survived to adulthood.

Following his release, Heyward was elected to the American Philosophical Society in 1784. The following year, he was one of the founders of the South Carolina Agricultural Society and was its first president.

In 1786, he married Elizabeth Savage, with whom he had three children. During these intervening years, he worked as a judge. In 1790, he was a delegate to the convention to draft a state constitution.

Thomas Heyward, Sr., Heyward's older brother, died in October 1795, after a painful illness that he handled with "Christian fortitude." Three years later, Heyward retired as a judge, and citing the pain from his war injuries, withdrew from public life soon after.

Heyward died on April 17, 1809, at the rebuild White Hall, in St. Luke's Parish (now Jasper County), South Carolina. He was buried at the Heyward Family Cemetery at "Old House," the site of the former White Hall. A marker near his tomb reads, "Tomb of Thomas Heyward,

Memorial of Thomas Heyward Jr.

Jr. 1746–1809. Member of South Carolina Provincial Congress and Council of Safety and of Continental Congress. Signer of Declaration of Independence and Articles of Confederation and captain of militia at Battle of Port Royal and Siege of Charleston. Prisoner of war 1780–81. Circuit Court Judge 1778–89."

In 1835, several newspapers heralded Heyward:

> He was at that a very young man, not more than twenty-five or thirty . . . he was, perhaps, the wealthiest planter in the Southern

## Thomas Heyward Jr. (1746–1809)

country. His estate consisted entirely of land and negroes [*sic*], a species of property very easily got hold of by the goods, he heard of the Declaration of Independence. To him, it appeared to be an act of great indiscretion, and altogether premature. The total conquest of the country, with a confiscation of all of the property belonging to the rebels, was to be, he feared, the sad result of this effort to throw off the yoke of the mother country . . . Thomas Heyward was one of the few Signers of the Declaration of Independence who returned home, and took up arms in defense of that Independence which they had declared . . . in fighting for his country, Thomas

Grave of Thomas Heyward Jr.

Heyward was severely wounded. He had the honor of sealing with his blood the written appeal which he had signed with his hand.

All white Heyward descendants alive today trace their lineage to the three children, Thomas, William, and Elizabeth, descended from the second wife. Thomas E. Miller (1849–1938) was the grandson of Heyward and a slave woman. Miller was one of five African American congressmen from the South in the 1890s.

Descendant DuBose Heyward's (1885–1940) novel *Porgy*, published in 1927, was used by George Gershwin to create *Porgy and Bess* in 1935, which critiqued racism.

It is estimated that Heyward's younger brother Nathaniel was the largest slaveholder in the United States with over 2,000 slaves working over 35,000 acres.

# Richard Hutson
# (1748–1795)

## First Mayor of Charleston

Buried at Circular Congregational Church Burying Ground, Charleston, South Carolina.

**Articles of Confederation**

Richard Hutson was a prominent lawyer, judge, and politician in Charleston, South Carolina. He was elected to the Second Continental Congresses and signed the Articles of Confederation. He also served as the eighth Lieutenant Governor of South Carolina and the first mayor of Charleston. He participated in the state constitutional convention to ratify the U.S. Constitution.

Richard Hutson was born July 9, 1748, in Prince William Parish, South Carolina, to Reverend William Hutson and his wife, Mary (née Woodward or Gibbes). The elder Hutson first studied law in England but disliked it. He came to America and as an actor in 1740, after which he was called to preach. Young Richard studied the classics. He then studied law and graduated from Princeton College in New Jersey in 1765. He was admitted to the South Carolina bar and opened a law practice in Charleston.

The young attorney was an early agitator for independence. He was elected to the provincial assembly in 1776. On January 18, 1777, he wrote Isaac Hayne, his brother-in-law, concerning the mood in South Carolina regarding a state religion:

Richard Hutson

The Dissenters' Petition came before the House on Saturday last. It was introduced and warmly supported by General Gadsden. In order to give you a general idea of the debates, it will be necessary to quote the paragraph, which it was the prayer of the Petition might be inserted into the [state] Constitution. It runs thus: That there shall never be any establishment of any one Denomination or sect of Protestants by way of preference to another in this State. That no Protestant inhabitant of this State shall, by law, be obligated to pay towards the maintenance and support of a religious worship that he does not freely join in or has not voluntarily engaged to support, nor to be denied the enjoyment of any civil right merely on account of his religious principles, but that all Protestants demeaning themselves peaceably under the government established under the constitution shall enjoy free and equal privileges, both religious and civil.

In early 1778, Christopher Gadsden, Arthur Middleton, Henry Laurens, and William Henry Drayton were elected to the Second Continental Congress. Middleton and Gadsden declined the honor, and a subsequent election for the three vacancies selected John Mathews, Thomas Heyward, Jr., and Richard Hutson. Wrote Historian David Duncan Wallace about the elections:

> During the spring and summer of 1778, Congress was considerably strengthened. [On] May 21st Samuel Adams returned from an absence of over six months, which, under the Massachusetts rule requiring three delegates, had deprived the State of her vote; Gouverneur Morris took his seat from New York [on] 20 January 1778; Roger Sherman returned [on] 25 April after a long absence. All the States, even Delaware at last, sent representatives; Laurens, who since the beginning of November 1777, had been the sole attendant from his State, was reinforced [on] 30 March by the brilliant young William Henry Drayton, [on] 13 April by Richard Hutson, [on] 22 April by John Matthews [sic; should be Mathews], and [on] 6 June by Thomas Heyward.

Hutson arrived at the Continental Congress when it was in York, Pennsylvania, having fled occupied Philadelphia. He served from April 13, 1778, until June 27, 1778. At that point, the Congress returned to Philadelphia. Hutson accompanied Elbridge Gerry and Francis Dana to Philadelphia by Wilmington and Chester, avoiding the public inns filled with other delegates and people returning to the city. The group crossed the Susquehanna at McCall's Ferry, southeast of York, and celebrated July 4th at City Tavern in Philadelphia. Hutson then served through February 26, 1779, during which he signed the Articles of Confederation on behalf of South Carolina.

Upon his return to Charleston in 1780, Hutson found himself on the front lines of a British invasion. When Charleston fell, he was captured along with Christopher Gadsden, Josiah Smith, Edward Blake, Jacob Read, and Alexander Moultrie. The group was taken by ship to St. Augustine, where they were held for many weeks.

Following his release, Hutson was elected to the state's Legislative Council, holding the position into 1782. Hutson had served in the South Carolina House of Representatives sporadically throughout the revolutionary years. In 1782, he was elected the lieutenant governor of the state and then, in 1783, was the first elected mayor of Charleston. In 1784, Hutson was elected to a court position, which he held until 1791. In 1788, he was a member of the state constitutional convention that ratified the U.S. Constitution. After 1791, Hutson was promoted to senior judge of the Chancery court.

Tomb of Richard Hutson.

## Richard Hutson (1748–1795)

Richard Hutson died in Charleston on April 12, 1795. He was buried in the Perrineau family vault in the Independent Congregational Church Cemetery, now the Circular Congregational Church Burying Ground, located in Charleston. A plaque placed on a wall next to his grave reads:

> Herein Lie the Remains of Richard Hutson 1747–1795. Son of Rev. William and Mary Woodward Hutson. South Carolina Patriot, Statesman, and Jurist. Graduated Princeton 1765. Founding Body the College of Charleston 1772–1794. Member S.C. General Assembly and Legislative Council 1776–1790. Served in Militia and Imprisoned by the British During the Revolutionary War. Delegate to the Continental Congress 1778–1779. Signer Articles of Confederation. Lieutenant Governor 1782–1783. Author of Act Incorporating City of Charleston 1783. First Intendant (Mayor) of Charleston 1783. Judge, Court of Chancery 1784–1794. Senior Judge 1791–1794.

# Francis Marion
## (1732–1795)

### Swamp Fox

Buried at Belle Isle Plantation Cemetery,
Berkeley County, South Carolina.

**Military**

Francis Marion, nicknamed the "Swamp Fox," was an officer in the South Carolina militia and the Continental Army during the American Revolution known by the enemy for his irregular methods of warfare. He was best known for his resistance to the British occupation of South Carolina late in the American Revolution. Marion is considered one of the fathers of modern guerilla warfare. He has been portrayed in books and movies since as an American hero.

Francis Marion was born in 1732, at Winyah near Georgetown, South Carolina, to Gabriel Marion, a country planter, and his wife, Esther Cordes. The Marions were of Huguenot ancestry who had been in the colonies since the 1600s. Francis was the youngest of seven children. According to Parson Weems, Marion was born so small; he was the size of a New England lobster.

Marion was not formally educated. As a teenager of fifteen or sixteen, he joined a West Indies-bound schooner. Likely an apocryphal tale, a few days out of Charleston, like an episode in *Moby Dick*, the ship was battered and sunk by a whale. Marion was among six crew members who drifted at sea for a week in a lifeboat. Two died before they were rescued

## Francis Marion (1732–1795)

Francis Marion

by a passing ship. Marion then focused on terrestrial pursuits at the family plantation, near the Santee River, about 45 miles north of Charleston.

As the French and Indian War commenced, Marion and his brother, Job, were recruited by Captain John Postell on January 1, 1757. In 1759, when the Cherokee rebelled against the British, Marion was elevated to a first lieutenant in a light infantry company. At the climactic Battle of Etchoe in June 1761, Marion led 30 men in an uphill flanking assault against a strong Cherokee position. Two-thirds of his men fell dead or wounded, but the attack secured a decisive victory and made Marion a hero.

Marion served as a local official after the war. In 1773, he built his plantation home, Pond Bluff, a few miles south of Eutaw Springs, South Carolina. The site is now beneath the waters of Lake Marion. In 1775, Marion was elected to the First Provincial Congress of South Carolina.

At the beginning of the American Revolution, in June 1775, Marion was commissioned a captain and company commander in the 2nd

Continental Regiment of South Carolina under William Moultrie. His ability to train raw recruits into a disciplined unit resulted in his promotion to major, second in command of the regiment.

During the early years of the Revolution, Marion participated in the major campaigns in South Carolina and Georgia. He took part in the capture of Fort Johnson in September 1775. At Sullivan's Island on June 28, 1776, Marion and 400 South Carolinians under Moultrie successfully defended against nine British warships in Charleston Harbor. This was especially remarkable since the fortification, built of palmetto logs, was only partially completed. The Continental Congress promoted Marion to lieutenant colonel in September 1776.

Three years later, in the summer and fall of 1779, Marion and his regiment were part of a French American force sent to retake Savannah, Georgia, from the British. His Second Regiment took part in a costly frontal assault against well-entrenched British and loyalist soldiers. The attack failed.

The British under Henry Clinton then moved on Charleston in the spring of 1780. Just before the British cut the last roads leading inland, Marion attended a party where the host locked his guests in until they were drunk. Marion, who was beyond his limit, decided to leave the party by jumping from a second-story window. The fall fractured his ankle, and he went home to recover. When Charleston fell, Marion was healing at home and was not captured. Meanwhile, Clinton returned with most of the army to New York, leaving Lord Cornwallis and a smaller force in the Carolinas.

The British, under Cornwallis, then began scouring the countryside. Despite his crippling injury, Marion fled to Horatio Gates's new American army assembling in North Carolina with a few fellow officers and comrades from his regiment. Gates found Marion an utterly unimpressive figure—short, scrawny, homely, taciturn, and so crippled by a poorly healed ankle fracture that his black manservant had to help him dismount from his horse. Before Gates engaged the enemy at Camden, Marion received a request from the residents of Williamsburg County, South Carolina, to come and help defend them. Marion, now a brigadier general in the militia, was permitted to go home and gather a small force.

## Francis Marion (1732–1795)

Colonel Otho Williams, Gates's adjutant, recorded afterward that the northern troops derided the appearance of Marion and his men. Gates seemed only too happy to send Marion and his ragtag group back to South Carolina. He ordered Marion to destroy all the watercraft along the Santee River below Camden before turning east to reach his destination above Charleston. Gates hoped that Marion's small force could frustrate British efforts to reinforce Camden and prevent their retreat after they were defeated. Unfortunately, Gates was defeated convincingly, and now Marion was on his own along the coast.

Between August and December 1780, Marion gained recognition for his actions across the region. While the British looted, burned, and forced captured rebels to switch sides, Marion countered with guerilla tactics and rough treatment of loyalists. Rarely did Marion make frontal assaults but instead relied on surprise attacks to harass and bewilder the enemy before disappearing into the swamp. The British's harsh treatment only increased the opportunities for groups led by Marion, Sumter, and Pickens to recruit and find supplies. Unlike the Continental troops, Marion's Men served without pay and supplied their own horses, arms, and food.

They fought at Great Savannah on August 20 and Blue Savannah on September 4. On September 24, learning that a force of Tories was constructing a small fort at Shepherd's Ferry on Black Mingo Creek, about 30 miles north of Georgetown, Marion planned a night attack. When the clatter of their horses' hooves on a bridge alerted an enemy sentry, Marion hurried his men across the stream, split them into three parties, and attacked from as many directions. But the Tories had received sufficient warning to deploy, and their initial volley caught part of Marion's force crossing an open field and inflicted severe casualties. A sharp fight ensued before one of Marion's other detachments attacked the Tories from the rear, killing and wounding many and scattering the rest.

After this battle, most of Marion's men returned to their homes to bring in the harvest while he was based at Snow's Island, located on the west side of the Great Pee Dee River, just below its confluence with Lynches River. It was further protected by a creek, a lake, and broad belts of cypress swamp and dense canebrakes. Marion used this naturally moated refuge as a supply depot, recruiting station, and sanctuary for the next six months. A British officer who was sent to arrange a prisoner exchange was picked up by Marion's men, blindfolded, and taken to the swampy hideout. There, Marion invited him to share his dinner of roasted sweet potatoes served upon plates of bark. "But surely, general," the officer objected, "this cannot be your ordinary fare."

"Indeed, sir, it is," Marion dryly replied, "and we are fortunate on this occasion, entertaining company, to have more than our usual allowance."

By late October 1780, enough men returned from the harvest so that Marion could resume operations. First up was a Tory recruiting base near the Black River. Marion took 150 men, covered 40 miles, crossed three rivers, and took the enemy's camp by surprise at midnight on October 25 at Tearcoat Swamp. When the Tories fled, Marion's men seized 80 new muskets and an equal number of horses and saddles.

There were also actions at Georgetown on November 15 and Halfway Swamp in mid-December 12–13.

Cornwallis was so concerned about Marion; he sent Banastre Tarleton's 800-man brigade out to capture him. Hearing this, Marion, realizing the long odds, released his men to their homes and headed to North Carolina.

Lieutenant Colonel Banastre Tarleton, known by the patriots as "The Butcher" and "Bloody Ban," led a force known as the British Legion. Tarleton was known for brutal tactics, often killing troops taken prisoner. He came after Marion with his legion and nearly blundered into Marion's brigade on the evening of November 9 at Richardson's Plantation near the Santee River. Each side discovered the other at the same moment. Marion's force was about half the size of Tarleton's, so he ordered a hasty retreat. The chase ensued through the night and onto the following day, November 10.

After riding 33 miles through swamps, creeks, thickets, and forests, Tarleton and his legion were now on the banks of Ox Swamp, near the town of Manning, with no sign of Marion. Frustrated, he turned to his officers and said, "Come, my boys! Let us go back, and we will soon find the gamecock [Sumter], but as for this damned old fox, the devil himself could not catch him." Thus, Marion's famous nickname, "Swamp Fox," was born.

## Francis Marion (1732–1795)

Wrote Lord Cornwallis to General Clinton in early December, "Colonel Marion had so wrought the minds of the people, partly by the terror of his threats and cruelty of his punishments, and partly by the promise of plunder, that there was scarcely an inhabitant between the Santee and the Pee Dee that was not in arms against us." The British turned their attention to protecting their communication lines between Charleston, Camden, and the frontier settlement known as Ninety-Six. They erected Fort Watson on the east side of the Santee, and Fort Motte, farther north, just west of the juncture of the Congaree and Wateree rivers. At this point, South Carolina's governor, John Rutledge, promoted Marion to brigadier general of state troops.

In early 1781, Marion was paired with "Light Horse" Harry Lee's Legion under Major General Nathanael Greene, who had replaced Horatio Gates. Unlike Thomas Sumter, Marion coordinated effectively in the field with the Continental Army. But Marion and Lee were an odd pair. At 25, Lee was outgoing and dashing. Marion was nearly fifty, hook-nosed, swarthy, bowlegged, and reserved. He drank a mixture of vinegar and water and was so indifferent to his appearance; he continued to wear his old leather 2nd Regiment cap even after it was partially burned.

After a failed raid on Georgetown, Lee rejoined Greene's army. This left Marion's brigade alone in March 1781 when Colonel Francis, Lord Rawdon, who had taken over when Lord Cornwallis moved north to pursue Greene's army, planned an attack on Snow's Island. Lieutenant Colonel John Watson and a force of 500 loyalists proceeded east from Fort Watson. Lieutenant Colonel Welbore Doyle and his 300 loyalists were sent east from Camden to cut off Marion from retreating to North Carolina. On March 7, Watson and Marion clashed at Wiboo Swamp, the British getting the worst of it. As they tried to outflank him, Marion anticipated their moves and caught them at a bridge over the Black River two days later. Seventy mounted riflemen destroyed the bridge before the British arrived and then shot at them from the trees, frustrating their attempts to cross. Watson ordered a retreat and headed to a nearby plantation, where he remained for ten days.

On March 15, Watson asked Marion for passes to remove his wounded to Charleston. Marion obliged but kept pressing. By March

20, Watson's troops were out of food, but Marion's riflemen prevented them from foraging. Facing a dire situation, Watson and his men bolted for Georgetown, thirty miles away. Marion sent a party of horsemen ahead to destroy the bridge on the Sampit River. Watson's men desperately plunged into the stream and splashed across as Marion's main force arrived. The Tories lost 20 killed and 38 wounded. Marion only lost a single man. The remnants of Watson's command limped into Georgetown the next day, its wagons loaded with wounded. Unfortunately, while battling Watson in what was known as "the Bridges Campaign," Colonel Doyle and his men destroyed Snow's Island and took all the weapons and ammunition. Doyle then retreated to Camden rather than face Marion.

After the Battle at Guilford Courthouse, General Greene turned his army back to South Carolina and reunited Lee and Marion. He ordered them to attack the British forts between Charleston and Camden. The first target was Fort Watson in April 1781. This same fort had withstood an attack by Thomas Sumter six weeks earlier. Without any cannons, the patriots laid siege for eight days and cleverly built wooden towers from which the sharpshooters could fire into the fort. Realizing their situation was hopeless, the British surrendered. Nathanael Greene wrote to Marion just after Fort Watson's fall, noting that Marion, despite fighting against superior foes, had kept "alive the expiring hopes of an oppressed militia. To fight the enemy bravely with the prospect of victory is nothing, but to fight with intrepidity under the constant impression of defeat, and to inspire irregular troops to do it, is a talent peculiar to yourself."

On April 25, Greene defeated Lord Rawdon at Hobkirk's Hill. After Lee and Marion took Fort Motte on May 12, Lord Rawdon ordered Camden abandoned, burning many of its buildings and supplies that he could not take. This broke the line of communications in the region for the British and further accelerated their collapse. After three more forts were captured, Marion and his men began to dig in at Georgetown, expecting a confrontation, but the British and loyalist garrison boarded three ships and sailed to Charleston, abandoning the town. This was a bloodless victory for Marion, who finally cleaned himself up and obtained a fresh uniform.

Marion continued to harass the British around Charleston through the summer. He commanded South Carolina militia in advance lines along with Brig. Gen. Andrew Pickens at the Battle of Eutaw Springs in September 1781, the last major battle in the Carolinas. The British suffered so many casualties they ceased further inland campaigning.

Over the next fifteen months, there were skirmishes between foraging parties on the outskirts of Charleston. In January 1782, Marion took a seat in the new South Carolina state assembly. He supported measures to foster reconciliation with the state's loyalists, on one occasion preventing his men from lynching a notorious Tory commander. Marion was very reluctant to attack the enemy for fear of losing another man wisely preferred to wait out the British. He said, "If ordered to attack, I shall obey, but with my consent, not another life shall be lost . . . Knowing, as we do, that the enemy are on the eve of departure, so far from offering to molest, I would rather send a party to protect them." The British evacuated Charleston in December 1782. The war ended with the Treaty of Paris.

The war had ruined Marion financially. His plantation had been burned, and his slaves had run away. He borrowed money to purchase more and restart planting. On April 20, 1786, he married his wealthy cousin, Mary Esther Videau. The two lived a comfortable life, but the two had no children.

Marion was awarded a gold medal, a full colonelcy in the Continental Army, and command of Fort Johnson in Charleston harbor. He served in the state Senate from 1783 to 1786, 1791, and 1792 to 1794. He was elected to the state constitutional convention in 1790. Marion also continued as a brigadier general in the militia until his retirement in 1794. At that point, he owned upward of eighteen hundred acres and seventy-three slaves.

Francis Marion died at Pond Bluff, his estate, on February 27, 1795. He was buried in the family plot at Belle Island in St. Stephen's Parish, Berkeley County, South Carolina. A plaque on his tomb aptly describes him as a "noble and disinterested" citizen and a soldier "who lived without fear and died without reproach."

The life of Francis Marion became somewhat legendary due to early biographies and novels that exaggerated his exploits. Marion was presented in the 1955 television show "The Swamp Fox," an episode of the *Cavalcade of America* series. Walt Disney then produced an eight-episode miniseries entitled *The Swamp Fox*. It aired from 1959 to 1961 and starred Leslie Nielsen. Marion was the inspiration for Benjamin Martin, played by Mel Gibson, in the 2000 movie *The Patriot*. Many historians criticized the many oversights and exaggerations in the film, television show, and early biographies.

Numerous towns, counties, parks, hotels, ships, and monuments were named or raised in Marion's honor. Congress approved a national monument to Francis Marion in 2008. Though the park was selected, the monument was never built due to some residents opposing a monument to a slaveowner. The authorization expired in 2018.

The tomb of Francis Marion, the Swamp Fox.

# John Mathews
## (1744–1802)

### "The Disagreeable One"

Buried at Circular Congregational Church Burying Ground, Charleston, South Carolina.

**Signer of Articles of Confederation • Continental Congress Governor • Militia**

John Mathews was a lawyer from Charleston, South Carolina, who was involved in politics. He served in local positions and was elected to the Continental Congress in time for the Articles of Confederation, which he signed. Near the end of the American Revolution, he was elected governor of South Carolina for one term. For the remainder of his life, he served in state judicial positions.

Mathews was born in 1744 in Charleston, South Carolina, the son of John Mathews and his wife, Sarah (née Gibbes). His paternal lineage was from Captain Anthony Mathewes (1661–1734), who emigrated to South Carolina from London in 1680.

Early in the 1760s, Mathews fought the Cherokee in South Carolina as an ensign in the South Carolina Provincial Regiment. He was promoted to lieutenant in the process.

Mathews next studied law and went to England, where he entered the Middle Temple in 1764. He graduated in 1766 and returned to South Carolina, where he initially clerked for Colonel Charles Pinckney before he was admitted to the colonial bar. However, Mathews did not

John Mathews

practice law in South Carolina. Rather, he became a politician, speaking against the various actions of the British Parliament following the French and Indian War.

In December 1766, Mathews married Mary Wragg, the half-sister of Charlotte Wragg, who married William Loughton Smith, a fellow delegate to the Continental Congress from South Carolina. The couple had no children. Mathew's sister, Elizabeth, was married to another Continental Congressman, Thomas Heyward Jr.

In 1772, Mathews was elected to the South Carolina Commons House of Assembly. There, he called for a boycott of British goods. From June 1774 until June 1775, Mathews was a member of the Committee of Ninety-Nine, which formed a rebel government in the colony. Mathews also returned to the military as a lieutenant in the provincial militia, guarding Fort Charlotte on the Savannah and Fort Moore near present-day Augusta.

During 1775 and 1776, following the hostilities commencing at Lexington and Concord, Mathews was appointed an associate judge on the state circuit court and a member of the First and Second Provincial Congresses in South Carolina. From 1776 to 1780, Mathews served in the South Carolina House of Representatives, serving as speaker in 1777 and 1778. He also continued his military service as a captain in the Colleton County regiment.

On January 22, 1778, after Christopher Gadsden and Henry Middleton declined to continue serving, Mathews was elected to the Continental Congress. He immediately found himself embroiled in the debates about the Articles of Confederation following the meetings in York, Pennsylvania. Mathews was unhappy from the start, describing the trip from South Carolina to York, Pennsylvania, "A most disagreeable journey, indeed." He followed this with a complaint about the indecision in Congress to John Rutledge on July 7, 1778:

> We are thrown into a good deal of confusion with regard to the Confederation. Before we left York-Town, Congress proceeded to the consideration of the amendments offered by the different States to the Confederation, every one of which have been rejected. It was then ordered to be engroced [*sic*] to [be] ready for ratification when we came to Philadelphia. Now, that it is so, Mr. Laurens, Mr. Drayton, and Mr. Hutson say they will not sign it because they do not think themselves authorized by our instructions to do so unless the other twelve states will agree to sign it likewise. Maryland has refused to ratify. Mr. Heyward and my self [*sic*] are of a different opinion, and think we are authorized, not withstanding [*sic*] one or even two States were to refuse, nor do I apprehend that inconsistancy [*sic*] will arise in the Confederation, from the Defection of one or two States which these three Gentlemen seem to imagine, however they mean, I believe, to write to the Prest. or to you, to be laid before the Assembly. I do not think it necessary for Heyward and myself to write on the subject, in our public Characters, as we think we are authorised [*sic*] to sign it, but as Three are necessary to a final Ratification, we must wait for your decision. This I am clear in, from what I have seen, and know, since I have been in Congress, that if we are to have no Confederation until the Legislatures of the Thirteen States agree to one, that we shall never

have one, and if we have not one, we shall be literally a rope of sand, and I shall tremble for the consequences that will follow at the end of this War.

Mathews quickly developed a reputation as a complainer in Congress. He did not enjoy his time in the sessions, complaining about his fellow Congressmen, "Those who have dispositions for jangling and are fond of displaying their Rhetorical abilities, let them come. I never was so sick of anything in my life." He wrote to others about his frustrations with the slow pace of things. Regardless of his mood, Mathews signed the Articles of Confederation on July 21, 1778. His complaints about his fellow members continued, and they also described his temperament as hot, "like the country of his nativity."

Mathews was reelected to the Congress in 1779 and 1780, joining Henry Laurens, Francis Kinloch, Arthur Middleton, and Thomas Bee as delegates from South Carolina. During his tenure, he served on the Committee of Congress, which dealt with military matters. When Mathews got word of Charleston's fall in 1780, he wished to return from Congress. Only John Rutledge, the governor, remained, now in exile in North Carolina. Britain was trying to pry away the Southern states from the rest, but the patriots would not hear it. Rutledge urged Mathews to stay in Congress to help manage affairs there.

After Nathanael Greene's victory at Eutaw Springs on September 9, 1781, the tide turned against the British, who now fell back to Charleston. Rutledge prepared for the re-establishment of South Carolina's government in late 1781. On January 24, 1782, the South Carolina House met and announced the return of John Mathews from Philadelphia. After both Christopher Gadsden and Richard Hutson were elected and declined the post of governor, Mathews was elected. The house voted that Mathews could not refuse the post! Mathews then retired from Congress and became the governor. He was sworn in on January 31, 1782, and served until February 4, 1783. During this time, the British evacuated Charleston in December 1782, and Mathews threatened the nonpayment of British merchants if the soldiers carried off any goods from the citizens of the city. The negotiation worked.

After his governorship, Mathews was a judge on the state Court of Chancery in 1784 and again served in the South Carolina House. He remained involved in Charleston's affairs and sold off his merchant sloop. He also advertised for a fugitive slave in August 1790, seeking the recovery of Jemmy "of the African country." Mathews was a judge on the state Court of Equity in 1791. He was also a founding trustee of the College of Charleston.

After Mary's passing, Mathews married Sarah Rutledge in May 1799. She was the sister of John and Edward Rutledge, both Continental Congressmen. The couple had no children.

Mathews followed his wife to the grave on October 30, 1802, in Charleston. He was buried at the Circular Congregational Church Burying Ground in Charleston.

# Arthur Middleton
## (1742–1787)

### Defender of Charleston

Buried at the gardens at "Middleton Place,"
Charleston, South Carolina.

---

**Declaration of Independence • Military**

Arthur Middleton was a signer of the Declaration of Independence and, along with his father, Henry, was a delegate to the Continental Congress (1776–77 and 1781–82). A wealthy plantation owner, Arthur was also a leading attorney in colonial South Carolina.

---

Arthur was born at "Middleton Place," his father's expansive estate along the Ashley River west of Charleston, South Carolina, on June 26, 1742. He was the son of Henry Middleton and Mary Baker Williams, both of English descent. Father Henry owned, at one point, 20 plantations comprising approximately 50,000 acres, worked by over 800 slaves.

Young Arthur was first taught by private tutors and schools in the Charleston area before traveling to England to attend Hackney (later Harrow), Westminster School, and Trinity Hall, Cambridge University, where he graduated in 1760 at the age of 18. He then studied law at the Middle Temple in London, before touring Europe for two years, acquiring a taste for music, painting, sculpture, and architecture. He enjoyed a prolonged stay in Rome, appreciating its ancient heritage. He returned home just before Christmas 1763, a well-educated and cultured Renaissance man.

## Arthur Middleton (1742–1787)

Portrait of Arthur Middleton from the detail from a 1771 family portrait of the Middleton Family. The full portrait depicts Arthur; his wife Mary Izard Middleton, and their infant son Henry. It was painted by Benjamin West.

On August 19, 1764, Middleton married Mary Izard, the daughter of his neighbor, Walter Izard, a plantation owner and captain of a Berkeley regiment in 1712 who also served in the Yemassee War. The young couple settled in at "Middleton Place" and produced nine children.

During his 20s, Arthur engaged in planting and became a justice of the peace Berkeley County in 1765 followed by election to the South Carolina House of Commons from 1765 to 1768 and again from 1772 to 1775.

Vehemently anti-Loyalist, Arthur was a member of the American Party in Carolina, a founding member of the Council of Safety in 1775 and 1776 (including its Secret Committee), and a delegate to the South Carolina Congress when it created its state constitution in 1776. Middleton wrote to William Henry Drayton on April 15, 1775:

You put me in mind of Cicero Parthians after the Surrender of Pindenissum. You may say with him 'take it however as a Certainty, that no one could do more than I have done with such an Army." I hope you will do great matters with your great Guns, & I wish your Second in Command was not quite so sleepy, it is pity you had not roused him with a discharge. If you should not find it hot enough up your way, pray hasten down for in all probability we shall have warm work here 'ere long. It is confidently said Transports & Frigates will be here soon. Col. Laurens writes you & I suppose will acquaint you with our late Transactions. Fort Johnson is in our hands, & garrisoned with 150 men, which will be reinforc'd this night.

Said Benjamin Rush of Middleton, "he was a man of cynical temper but upright intentions towards his country." Others described him, variously, as being middle-sized, well-formed with great muscular strength and fine features expressive of firmness and decision, a celebrated, capricious aristocrat but like his forbears very public-spirited. Middleton had great disdain for Loyalists and assisted in the confiscation of the estates of those who had fled the country. He also participated in the tarring and feathering of those who remained.

Middleton succeeded his father when elected to the Continental Congress from 1776 to 1777 during which he proudly signed the Declaration of Independence. He served again in the Congress from 1781 to 1782. This entire time, from 1776 through 1786, he was also a justice of the peace in South Carolina.

During the Revolution, Middleton served as an officer in the local militia in the defense of Charleston. As the British scoured the countryside, they plundered plantations, grabbing anything that they could carry. The Middletons fled to Charleston ahead of the troops. During this time, the British plundered his estate including over 200 slaves, which were sold in the West Indies. After the city's fall to the British in 1780, he was a prisoner, along with Edward Rutledge and Thomas Heyward, Jr., from May 1780 to July 1781 in St. Augustine, Florida, until exchanged. Wife Mary begged, to no avail, for help from the British to care for her nine children.

## Arthur Middleton (1742–1787)

During his imprisonment, Arthur was again elected to the Continental Congress. He was reelected on 4 October 4, 1781, and again on January 31, 1782. A note from Daniel of St. Thomas Jenifer to John Hall, July 24, 1781, mentioned the freed patriots, "Ned [sic] Rutledge, Middleton, and Gadsden with many others exchanged are dayly [sic] expected from Augustine."

Middleton left the Congress before his term was out and returned home to "Middleton Place" where he focused on restoring his plantation and South Carolina affairs. Governor John Rutledge, the brother of his cellmate Edward Rutledge, appointed him to the state senate. He was re-elected to the seat in 1782. He was a member of the privy council that year and subsequently a member of the state house of representatives in 1785 and 1786. He was also a member of the board of trustees of Charleston College.

Middleton passed away suddenly on January 1, 1787, at the age of 44 at one of the Middleton plantations, "The Oaks." He was interred in the family mausoleum in the gardens at "Middleton Place," near Charleston, South Carolina, where he rests to this day. The *State Gazette of South Carolina* of January 4, 1787, included a notice about Middleton, describing him as a "tender husband and parent, humane master, steady unshaken patriot, the gentleman, and the scholar." He left behind a wife, eight children, "an untarnished name," and 600 slaves.

Historian Alexander Garden wrote in 1828:

The rebuilt "Middleton Place" as it looks today (photo by Lawrence Knorr).

I know no man, whose exemplary conduct, throughout the whole progress of the Revolution, deserves more gratefully to be remembered, than that of Arthur Middleton. Possessed of ample fortune, and endowed with talents of the highest order, improved by study, and refined by traveling, he devoted himself with decision to the service of his country . . . He, on all occasions, advocated the most vigorous measures, clearly evincing that he was not one of those, who shrunk in times of danger from responsibility. Frank and open to temper, he freely uttered the bold conceptions of his ardent spirit, censuring with indignant pride the cautious policy of the timid and irresolute, and expressing the highest indignation at the arts of the designing.

Among Middleton's heirs included his son Henry Middleton (1770–1846), who served as Governor of South Carolina (1810–12), in the U.S. House of Representatives (1815–19), and as U.S. minister to Russia (1820–30), and his daughter Emma Philadelphia Middleton (1776–1813), who married U.S. Senator Ralph Izard (1741/42–1804).

The grave of Arthur Middleton in the lovely gardens at "Middleton Place" near Charleston, South Carolina (photo by Lawrence Knorr).

## Arthur Middleton (1742–1787)

His grandson, Williams Middleton (1809–1883), signed the Ordinance of Secession that separated South Carolina from the Union and launched the American Civil War in 1861. Arthur Middleton's son-in-law was Congressman Daniel Elliott Huger who was the grandfather-in-law of Confederate General Arthur Middleton Manigault who was also a descendant of Henry Middleton. Arthur Middleton was also an ancestor of actor Charles B. Middleton, who played Ming the Merciless in the Flash Gordon movies of the 1930s.

The plantation passed to Henry, his eldest son, but it was burned and pillaged by Union troops during the Civil War. Today, "Middleton Place" is a historic landmark. A mansion was rebuilt and the grounds, including the Middleton gardens, are open to the public.

Arthur Middleton has been remembered in other ways. The United States Navy ship, USS *Arthur Middleton* (AP-55/APA-25), was named for him. Middleton's signature and those of all the signers of the Declaration of Independence are carved on granite rocks in a lagoon near the Washington Monument. The famous Trumbull painting "The Declaration of Independence" hangs in the U.S. Capitol. The figure of Arthur Middleton is shown standing in a group of five delegates on the left side of the painting, on the extreme right of the group, with his head tilted forward.

# Henry Middleton
## (1717 – 1784)

### "The Interim President"

Buried at St. James Goose Creek Cemetery,
Goose Creek, South Carolina

**Continental Association**

Henry Middleton was a signer of the Continental Association during his service in the Continental Congress from 1774-1776 as a delegate from South Carolina. He also briefly served as the second President of Congress. Middleton was a wealthy plantation owner and the father of Declaration of Independence signer Arthur Middleton. However, after the fall of Charleston in 1780, he reaffirmed his loyalty to the king and remained a British subject until his death in 1784.

Middleton was born on his father Arthur Middleton's plantation, "The Oakes" near Charleston, South Carolina, in 1717. He was the son of Arthur and Sarah (née Amory) Middleton. The Middleton line had likely originated near Derbyshire, England, as far back as Queen Elizabeth I. Arthur (the elder) served in the colonial government including rising to acting governor. Middleton was likely taught by private tutors at home before going to England to complete his education.

During his younger years, Middleton served as a justice of the peace and later was elected to the colonial Commons of the Hour of Assembly, representing his St. George's County. In 1754, he was elected Speaker of

# Henry Middleton (1717 – 1784)

Portrait of Henry Middleton by Benjamin West, circa 1771.

this body and was later named as a member of His Majesty's Council for the Province of South Carolina.

Middleton married Mary Baker Williams with whom he had a dozen children, seven of whom survived childhood. Upon marrying Mary Williams in 1741, the daughter of John Williams, also a wealthy plantation owner, Middleton received a dowry which included the plantation that would become "Middleton Place." He and the family lived there until Mary's death in 1761, at which time he moved back to "The Oakes" and gave "Middleton Place" to his son Arthur. After Mary died, he married Mary Henrietta Bull, the daughter of William Bull, who had been the Lieutenant Governor of South Carolina. She died in 1772. The two had no children together, Middleton last married Lady Mary McKenzie in 1776.

Early on, Middleton was against the Stamp Act, and by 1770 had declined to continue serving on His Majesty's Council. In 1774, he was elected to the first Continental Congress, representing South Carolina along with John Rutledge, Christopher Gadsden, Thomas Lynch, and

Edward Rutledge, Middleton attended the entire first Continental Congress and into the second, until early 1776 when he became ill and was replaced by his son Arthur. Middleton had also been elected President of Congress for a brief period, October 22 to 26, in 1775 while Peyton Randolph was unable to serve. However, some records seem to indicate he might have served longer, starting earlier in October. A petition to Ben Franklin and others had been signed by Middleton, as President of Congress, as early as October 6.

During his service, Middleton had been instrumental in establishing a new government for South Carolina and was well-respected by others for his willingness to negotiate with the King as opposed to leaping right to independence like others from the northern colonies. In this regard, he differed from his son, who was a staunch voice for independence. Middleton resigned from his position in the Congress and returned to "The Oakes" prior to the Declaration of Independence due to declining health. His son signed the document instead.

As one of the leaders of the revolt against British rule, Middleton came to the attention to the British authorities, who ordered his arrest and execution. From a letter from the Earl of Dunmore from London, 30 January 1775:

> From unquestionable authority I learn, that about a fortnight ago, dispatches were sent hence by a sloop of war to General [Thomas] Gage, containing, among other things, a Royal Proclamation, declaring the inhabitants of Massachusetts Bay and some others, in the different Colonies, actual rebels; with a blank commission to try and execute such of them as he can hold of . . . with this is sent a list of names, to be inserted in the commission as he may judge expedient. I do not know them all, but Messrs. Samuel Adams, John Adams, Robert Treat Paine, and John Hancock, of Massachusetts Bay; John Dickinson, of Philadelphia; Peyton Randolph, of Virginia, and Henry Middleton, of South Carolina, are particularly named, with many others. This blacklist, the General will, no doubt, keep to himself, and unfold it gradually, as he finds it convenient.

## Henry Middleton (1717–1784)

Back in South Carolina, during the period between royal rule and statehood, Middleton was a member of the state Legislative Council, which helped to form South Carolina. In 1778 he was elected to the South Carolina state Senate, where he served until 1780.

When Charleston fell to the British in 1780, Middleton was faced with financial ruin and certain execution. Rather than face such an end, he paid off the British invaders and reaffirmed his loyalty. Subsequently, his estates were not further touched, though his son's was burned to the ground and ransacked.

Middleton's health continued to decline over the following years. He died in Charleston on June 13, 1784, after a long illness. He was laid

The graves of Henry Middleton's daughter Susannah Middleton and her husband Continental Congressman John Parker at St. James Goose Creek Cemetery in Goose Creek, South Carolina. The location of Henry's grave is not known, but it may be close to this one. Based on the old etching, there was a tombstone next to it that no longer exists. (photo by Lawrence Knorr).

to rest at St. James Goose Creek cemetery at "Goose Creek," one of the Middleton family estates, located in Berkeley County, South Carolina. In all, through purchases and other means, Middleton, by the time of his death, had accumulated some 50,000 acres of land, a total of 50 estates and plantations, and approximately 800 slaves, becoming one of the wealthiest men in South Carolina prior to and during the American Revolution.

Apparently, his reversal of loyalty did not diminish the opinions held of him locally due to his many contributions early in the fight for independence and the role played by his son, Arthur. His estates were not confiscated as were many loyalists following the war.

# William Moultrie
## (1730 – 1805)

### Hero of Sullivan's Island

Buried at Fort Moultrie Grounds,
Charleston, South Carolina.

**Military Commander • Governor**

William Moultrie was an American slave-owning planter and politician who became a general in the American Revolutionary War. He became a war hero when he successfully defended Charleston during the Battle of Sullivan's Island on June 28, 1776, in which he dealt the Royal Navy a crushing defeat. After the war, Moultrie returned to the South Carolina General Assembly in 1783. Two years later, he was elected Governor. In 1792, he was again elected governor. Fort Moultrie is named in his honor.

William Moultrie was born in Charleston, South Carolina, on November 23, 1730, to Dr. John and Lucretia Cooper Moultrie. His father was a prominent physician, exceptionally skilled in obstetrics. Little is known about William's early life and education, other than that he was baptized in December 1730 and married in 1749 at the age of 19. He married Damaris Elizabeth de St. Julien, a wealthy descendant of French immigrants whose family owned a large plantation. The couple had three children, one dying in infancy. Because of English laws that denied married women's rights to control property, he became an influential

MAJOR GENER<sup>L</sup>. WILLIAM MOULTRIE.

member of his community. He soon purchased a 1020-acre plantation and owned about 200 slaves.

In 1752, he was elected to the South Carolina Commons House of Assembly, beginning a political career that lasted until 1794. In 1758, after a decade of tension between the colonists and the Cherokee tribe, war broke out. Moultrie was appointed a captain of the South Carolina militia. He was active in the invasion of Cherokee County and rose to the rank of colonel in 1774.

As the revolution approached, Moultrie was chosen as a delegate to the First Continental Congress; however, he declined to serve. Instead, Moultrie stayed in South Carolina serving as deputy to both the First and Second South Carolina Provincial Congresses. He was a member of the First South Carolina General Assembly after the adoption of the state constitution in 1776. During this time, he was a staunch patriot and supporter of the revolutionary cause.

In 1776, the British mounted an attack on Charleston, the fourth-largest port in the colonies. Moultrie defended a small fort on Sullivan's Island at the entrance to Charleston Harbor. On June 28, 1776, the British attacked Sullivan's Island. Against impossible odds and outnumbered 2,200 British troops to 435 soldiers within the fort, Moultrie successfully prevented land and sea invasions of Charleston. The small fort on Sullivan's Island was named Fort Moultrie in his honor, and the Continental Congress passed a resolution thanking Moultrie. He was promoted to brigadier general, and his regiment was taken into the Continental Army.

In February 1779, at the Battle of Beaufort, Moultrie commanded a largely militia force and defeated the British. This boosted patriot morale after the British capture of Savannah, Georgia. In the spring of 1779, Major General Benjamin Lincoln, the commander of the Continental Army's Southern Department, took the bulk of the Southern Army to threaten Augusta, Georgia. Seizing the initiative, the British advanced on Charleston from Savannah. Moultrie led a skillful withdrawal from Black Swamp, where Lincoln had left him with a small force. That small force garrisoned Charleston and held off a brief British siege before Lincoln's force returned.

In the spring of 1780, a series of engagements led to the surrender of Charleston by General Lincoln and the capture of more than 5,000 Continental soldiers, the largest loss during the war. Moultrie was one of them, and he was left in command of the American prisoners and frequently negotiated on their behalf for better conditions.

# SOUTH CAROLINA PATRIOTS

While a prisoner, Lord Charles Montague, the British Governor of South Carolina, offered an opportunity to desert to the British to regain his freedom and lost property. He replied to Montague, "Could I be guilty of so much baseness I should hate myself and shun mankind?" He was exchanged for British General John Burgoyne in 1782. When he returned to American lines, Congress made him a major general.

After the war, Moultrie returned to the General Assembly in 1783. Two years later, the new State Legislature elected him Governor of South Carolina. He served until 1787, and because the South Carolina Constitution prevented governors from serving two consecutive terms,

Grave of William Moultrie

he was elected to the state senate in 1787. During this time, he served as a member of the South Carolina Convention to ratify the US Constitution. He again served as governor starting in 1792 and ending in 1794. He ran again for governor in 1798 but lost decisively to Federalist Edward Rutledge.

Financial misadventures left Moultrie practically destitute in his later years. Yet, in 1802, he managed to publish his papers as the two-volume *Memoirs of the American Revolution*. This important primary source is often quoted in other works and is still regarded as one of the best personal accounts of the Revolutionary War.

William Moultrie died on September 27, 1805, in Charleston, South Carolina, at the age of 74. His slaves had a varied and complex fate, as some were sold to settle debts, some were hired out to work for the Santee Canal Company, and some escaped.

Moultrie was initially buried in the family cemetery. His remains were later moved to Fort Moultrie in 1978.

# Andrew Pickens
## (1739 – 1817)

### The Wizard Owl

Buried at Old Stone Church Cemetery,
Clemson, Pickens County, South Carolina.

---

**Military**

This founder was a Revolutionary War South Carolina Militia General. He initially led troops against the Cherokee Indians in the French and Indian War and later against the British during the American Revolution. He was largely successful in both cases, though at one point he was captured by the British. The Continental Congress honored him for his service by awarding him a sword. Though he had fought Native Americans after the war, the sides mended fences, and he was held in high regard. The Indians he dealt with gave him the name Skyagunsta, "The Wizard Owl," a name said to be based on a highly regarded previous chief of the Cherokee. The nickname resulted from his ability to exploit the weaknesses of those he faced in battle. He was elected to the third United States Congress. His name was Andrew Pickens.

---

Pickens was born in 1739 in Bucks County, Pennsylvania. His parents were immigrants who had come to America from what is now Northern Ireland. The Pickens family moved from Pennsylvania following the Great Wagon Road that took them to Virginia's Shenandoah Valley. In 1752, they moved again, settling on the South Carolina frontier.

## Andrew Pickens (1739–1817)

Andrew Pickens

Pickens moved to Abbeville County, South Carolina, where he purchased land in 1764. The following year, he married Rebecca Calhoun, and they started a family. It was here that Pickens became acquainted with the Cherokee Indians. He built the Hopewell Plantation on the Keowee River. Just across the river was a Cherokee settlement known as Seneca.

Pickens' military career began during the Anglo-Cherokee War, which was part of the French and Indian War. The conflict broke out in 1758, when the Virginia militia attacked the Cherokees for the alleged theft of horses. Pickens was a member of the South Carolina militia and served in the war in 1760 and 1761.

When the American Revolution began, Pickens was a captain in the militia. The Cherokee had allied with the loyalists, and Pickens emerged as a military leader fighting them at Long Cane. On February 14, 1779, Pickens, who was now a colonel, led his 300-man militia against a Loyalist force of approximately 800 under Colonel James Boyd at the Battle of Kettle Creek in Georgia. As described by Rick Atkinson in his work *The Fate of the Day: The War for America, Fort Ticonderoga to Charleston, 1777-1780*, Pickens, despite being outnumbered, ordered a frontal lunge accompanied by attacks on both flanks. During the fighting, Boyd fell mortally wounded. On his deathbed, Boyd asked Pickens to send his wife a brooch he had saved for her. When she received it, she exclaimed, "It's a lie. No damned rebel ever killed my husband." But not only had her husband been killed, Pickens and his troops had killed sixty others as well, while losing nine of their own. The rebels had also captured more than 150 men and six hundred horses. Pickens described the victory as "the severest check and chastisement the Tories ever received in Georgia or South Carolina." The outcome of the battle slowed the successful recruitment of Loyalists.

In 1780, things did not go as well for Pickens. The British defeated the Southern Continental Army in the Siege of Charleston. Pickens surrendered a fort in the Ninety-Six District. He and his 300-man militia were captured and then paroled after taking an oath to sit out the war. For Pickens, the oath proved to be of a short duration. Tories destroyed much of his property and frightened his family. At this point, he informed the British that they had violated the terms of his parole, and he rejoined the war, serving with Francis Marion and Thomas Sumter.

After his return to the fighting, Pickens saw action in several engagements, including the Battle of Cowpens. The battle took place in Cowpens, South Carolina. Brigadier General Daniel Morgan led the Americans. The British troops were under the command of Lieutenant Colonel Banastre Tarleton. Tarleton had a simple plan: he would have his infantry attack Morgan directly while dragoon units would protect his left and right flanks. He would use his two-hundred-man cavalry to attack the Americans when they broke and ran.

Shortly before sunrise on January 17, 1781, the attack began. Morgan had given Pickens command of the militia. When the British soldiers reached the militia, they were greeted by two volleys of fire, with commanders specifically targeted. This resulted in forty percent of the British casualties being officers, leaving the attackers surprised and confused. As planned, Pickens' men seemed to flee after firing the second volley. Tarleton believed he was seeing a hasty retreat. He ordered his men to charge, and the Americans drew them into a double envelopment. Pickens' militia had reorganized and charged. The British forces were soundly defeated. South Carolina Governor John Rutledge promoted Pickens to brigadier general, and Congress awarded him a sword.

After the American victory in the Revolution, Pickens was elected to the South Carolina House of Representatives. During the winter of 1785/86, negotiations took place for 45 days at his Hopewell Plantation

Grave of Andrew Pickens

involving representatives of the United States and leaders of the Cherokee, Choctaw and Chickasaw Indians. This resulted in three agreements, each one known as the Treaty of Hopewell. The treaties defined boundaries between tribal lands and those opened for settlement. They included provisions for the exchange of prisoners, punishment of crimes against Native Americans and the regulation of trade.

Pickens served in the Third United States Congress from 1793 to 1795. He was an anti-administration member who opposed the policies championed by the Secretary of the Treasury, Alexander Hamilton. He was one of nine representatives, and the only member of the anti-administration party, to vote against the Eleventh Amendment to the United States Constitution. This amendment restricts the ability of individuals to sue in federal court the states in which they are not citizens.

Pickens passed away in South Carolina on August 11, 1817. He was laid to rest in the Old Stone Church Cemetery in Clemson, South Carolina. One of his descendants, Marion Scherger, wrote a children's book titled *Courageous Uncle Andrew: The Story of Andrew Pickens, Revolutionary War Hero*, that quotes from a journal written by Pickens' sister, Katherine, on the day he died. She wrote, "My brother was a Revolutionary War Hero, a successful merchant, planter, respected judge and legislator. However, my brother Andrew, as a man of honor, I will miss you."

Pickens' heroics in the Revolution serve as one of the models for the fictional character Benjamin Martin in the film *The Patriot*. In one scene, Martin asks the militia for two rounds prior to retreating, similar to the orders Pickens and his men carried out in the Battle of Cowpens.

# Charles Pinckney
## (1757 – 1824)

### Proponent of Slavery

Buried at St. Philip's Episcopal Church Cemetery, Charleston, South Carolina.

**U.S. Constitution • Military**

Charles Pinckney was a politician from South Carolina who served in the House of Representatives, the Senate, represented South Carolina at the Constitutional Convention, and was a signer of the Constitution. He was first cousin once-removed of fellow signer Charles Cotesworth Pinckney. Times were such that Pinckney dedicated his considerable political talents to the establishment of a strong national government so that as he put it "the effects of the revolution may never cease to operate, but continue to serve as an example to others until they have unshackled all the nations that have firmness to resist the fetters of despotism." Yet, Pinckney saw slavery as a positive good and could not imagine blacks as equals. He fought for the protection of the slave trade at the Constitutional Convention and, thirty years later, opposed the Missouri Compromise because it set the dangerous precedent of allowing the federal Congress to outlaw slavery in the territories.

Charles Pinckney was born on October 26, 1757, in Charleston, South Carolina. He was the son of Charles Pinckney and Frances Brewton, members of South Carolina's social elite. Pinckney's father

# SOUTH CAROLINA PATRIOTS

Portrait of Charles Pinckney etched by
Albert Rosenthal, 1888.

Colonel Pinckney was one of the colony's leading attorneys. Young Charles was tutored in Charleston in preparation for studying law in England but when the time came, his parents decided he should remain at home and study law in his father's office due to the growing unrest between the colonies and Great Britain.

He started to practice law in 1779 in Charleston and about that time he enlisted in the South Carolina militia. He became a lieutenant and served at the siege of Savannah in the fall of 1779. Shortly thereafter, the British initiated a campaign resulting in the capture of Charleston in May 1780. The young lieutenant was captured and held as a prisoner until June 1781. He was confined on the prison ship *Pack Horse* in Charleston harbor. The elder Pinckney was captured and pressured to swear allegiance to the crown, which he did in order to save his estate.

## Charles Pinckney (1757–1824)

After spending most of the summer of 1781 as a prisoner of war, Lieutenant Pinckney was among a group of officers exchanged through a general agreement. Upon returning home, he was elected to the Continental Congress. He first came to national prominence in May of 1786. At that time, he introduced a motion in Congress to reorganize completely the structure of the central governing body. In doing this he joined with Washington, Hamilton, and Madison in acknowledging the weaknesses and inadequacies of the Articles of Confederation. Through Pinckney's motion, the Continental Congress established a committee, heard from the states additional calls for reform, and eventually called for a meeting of delegates from all of the states to either reform the Articles or draft an entirely new governing document.

Pinckney was chosen to represent South Carolina at the Convention in Philadelphia in 1787. His role in the convention is controversial. Although one of the youngest delegates, he later claimed to have been the most influential and contended that he had submitted a draft that was the basis of the final Constitution. This was strongly disputed by James Madison and some other framers and rejected by most historians. Historians do however recognize that he was one of the leaders, he attended full time, spoke often (over 100 times) and effectively, and contributed immensely to the final draft and to the resolution of problems that arose during the debates. His major contributions were:

- The elimination of religious testing as a qualification to office.
- The division of the legislature into House and Senate.
- The power of impeachment being granted only to the House.
- The establishment of a single chief executive, who will be called President.
- The power of raising an army and navy being granted to Congress.
- The prohibition of states to enter into a treaty or to establish interfering duties.
- The regulation of interstate and foreign commerce being controlled by the national government.

When the issue of slavery arose, Pinckney stood among his fellow southerners in defense of the institution. He openly questioned the assertion that slavery was wrong. He stated that South Carolina would reject the Constitution if the document prohibited slave importation.

He signed the Constitution in September of 1787 and returned home to marry Mary Eleanor Laurens on April 27, 1788. The couple had three children.

In 1788, he served as floor manager for the nationalist forces in the state's convention that ratified the Constitution and then chaired a second assembly that drafted a new state constitution along the lines laid out in Philadelphia. In between, he won the first of several terms as governor.

In 1798 Pinckney was appointed to fill an unexpired term in the United States Senate. In the presidential election of 1800, he remained

Grave of Charles Pinckney at Saint Philips Episcopal Church Cemetery in Charleston, South Carolina (photo by Lawrence Knorr).

loyal to Thomas Jefferson, serving as his campaign manager in South Carolina and helping to carry the state for Jefferson. The victorious Jefferson appointed Pinckney as Minister to Spain (1801-1805), in which capacity he struggled valiantly but unsuccessfully to win cession of Florida to the United States.

Charles Pinckney returned to Charleston in January 1806 and again served in the South Carolina General assembly. In December of that year, he was elected to his fourth and final term as governor. He served again in the legislature from 1810 to 1814 and then temporarily withdrew from politics. In 1818 he ran and won election to the U.S. House of Representatives where he fought against the Missouri Compromise as he was interested in the expansion of slavery into new territories and states.

In 1821, Pinckney's health began to fail and he retired from politics. He died on October 29, 1824, just three days after his 67th birthday. He was buried in St. Philips Episcopal Church Cemetery in Charleston. A portion of his estate is now preserved as the Charles Pinckney National Historic Site.

# Charles Cotesworth Pinckney
## (1746–1825)

## XYZ Affair

Buried at St. Michael's Churchyard,
Charleston, South Carolina.

**Military • Diplomat • US Constitution**

Charles Cotesworth Pinckney was a South Carolina aristocrat who served as an officer in the Continental Army and later signed the US Constitution. He then served as the US Minister to France, ran once for vice president (1800), and ran twice for president as the Federalist candidate, losing to Thomas Jefferson (1804) and then James Madison (1808).

Pinckney was born on February 25, 1746, in Charleston, South Carolina, the son of the wealthy planter Charles Pinckney, later the colonial Chief Justice of South Carolina, and his wife, Eliza (née Lucas) Pinckney, a planter and agriculturalist who helped develop indigo cultivation in the area. Younger brother Thomas Pinckney and first cousin Charles Pinckney both later served as Governors of South Carolina.

From 1753 to 1758, the elder Pinckney was the colony's agent to England and the family lived in London. The elder Pinckney lobbied Parliament and the Court on behalf of the South Carolina planters. The Pinckney boys were enrolled in the Westminster School and remained when the family returned to South Carolina. Pinckney studied at Christ Church, Oxford, in 1763 and studied law at Middle Temple in 1764. He

## Charles Cotesworth Pinckney (1746–1825)

Charles Cotesworth Pinckney

next studied botany for a year, assisting French botanist André Michaux, for which he was honored by having a plant species named for him: *Pinckneya pubens*. He also studied chemistry in France before attending the prestigious military academy at Caen. He completed his studies in 1769 when he was admitted to the English bar. He briefly practiced law in England before starting legal practice in Charleston.

In 1770, Pinckney was elected to the colonial legislature, representing St. John's Colleton Parish. He also became a vestryman and warden for the Episcopal church and by 1772, was a lieutenant in the militia, eventually rising to colonel.

In 1773, Pinckney served as a regional attorney general. On September 28, 1773, he married Sarah Middleton, the daughter of Henry Middleton, who later was a President of Congress, and sister of Arthur Middleton, a signer of the Declaration of Independence. Together, they had four children and Pinckney was now connected to the South Carolina gentry involved in the Revolution, including the Middletons, Rutledges, and William Henry Drayton.

As the Revolution neared, Pinckney was a member of the new South Carolina provincial congress, replacing the colonial body. He participated in the various revolutionary committees and prepared Charleston's defense. After the Battles of Lexington and Concord, he volunteered for service in the Continental Army. As captain, he was the senior commander of the Grenadiers of the 1st South Carolina Regiment. When British General Sir Henry Clinton attacked Charleston by sea in June 1776, Pinckney helped lead the defense in the Battle of Sullivan's Island, though he did not participate directly. Later that year, Pinckney was promoted to colonel and took control of the entire regiment.

Wanting to be in the action, in 1777, Pinckney took his regiment north to Philadelphia to join General Washington. He arrived in time to participate in the Battles of Brandywine and Germantown. During this time, he met Alexander Hamilton and James McHenry, who later became important political allies.

The following year, Pinckney headed South, participating in the successful repulse of Loyalist militia and British regulars in Florida. However, the Patriots failed to reach St. Augustine due to logistical problems and were defeated at the Battle of Alligator Creek Bridge. Due to disease and disorganization, only half of the Patriot forces made it home.

Later, in 1778, Major General Benjamin Lincoln was sent south to defend Savannah, Georgia, from British occupation. Lincoln placed Pinckney in charge of his Continental brigades. In October 1779, Pinckney participated in an American and French attack on Savannah that failed, resulting in numerous casualties.

In 1780, at Fort Moultrie, Pinckney defended Charleston from a British attack. Unfortunately, on May 7, the fort fell and Charleston was captured on May 12, when Lincoln surrendered 5,000 men. Both Pinckney and General William Moultrie were placed under house arrest, and the British attempted to lure them away. Said Pinckney at this time, "If I had a vein that did not beat with the love of my Country, I myself would open it. If I had a drop of blood that could flow dishonorable, I myself would let it out."

## Charles Cotesworth Pinckney (1746–1825)

Pinckney remained in captivity until he was exchanged in Philadelphia in 1782. Upon his release, he rejoined the army, but the fighting had ended. At the conclusion of hostilities in November 1783, he was breveted to brigadier general.

Sadly, his wife, Sarah, died in 1784. The following year, Pinckney was wounded in a duel with Daniel Huger, leading him to advocate for anti-dueling laws. In 1786, Pinckney married Mary Stead, a daughter of wealthy Georgia planters. The couple had three daughters.

Pinckney returned to his legal practice and a seat in the South Carolina legislature, where he and his brother Thomas became political powers who advocated for the slave-owning gentry. He opposed Edward Rutledge's attempt to end the importation of slaves out of concern for the South Carolina economy. He was also involved in resolving the border with Georgia and signed the Convention of Beaufort to that effect. Regarding his militia service, Pinckney was promoted to major general of one of two divisions of the South Carolina militia.

In favor of a stronger central government, Pinckney represented South Carolina at the Constitutional Convention in 1787, along with younger cousin Charles Pinckney and two others. He argued to include slaves to be counted for the basis of representation and claimed that the Northwest Ordinance of July 1787 permitted slaveowners to reclaim their fugitives anywhere in the new nation. Boasted Pinckney, "We have obtained a right to recover our slaves in whatever part of America they may take refuge, which is a right we had not before."

Pinckney believed it impractical to elect representatives by popular vote and felt senators, as members of the wealthy gentry, need not be paid. He also played a key role in requiring treaties to be ratified by the Senate and in the continuation of the slave trade for another twenty years, extending it to 1808. Said Pinckney about slavery, "While there remained one acre of swampland uncleared of South Carolina, I would raise my voice against restricting the importation of negroes . . . the nature of our climate and the flat, swampy situation of our country, obliges us to cultivate our lands with negroes, and that without them South Carolina would soon be a desert waste . . ." However, he recognized the irony of our founding documents when he said, "Bills of rights generally begin with declaring that all men are by nature born free. Now, we should make that declaration with a very bad grace, when a large part of our property consists in men who are actually born slaves."

He also wanted no limitation placed on the size of the federal standing army.

Pinckney played a prominent role in ratifying the new Constitution in South Carolina in 1788. When the new President, George Washington, offered him his choice of the War Department or State Department in 1789, Pinckney declined both. Instead, he focused on the framing of a new state constitution in 1790. He then retired from politics and devoted himself to religious and charitable works, including establishing a state university, improving the Charleston library, and promoting scientific agriculture. The town and district of Pinckneyville in South Carolina were named in his honor in 1791. He was also appointed to the American Philosophical Society in 1789.

In 1796, Pinckney accepted President Washington's call to be the Minister to France following the Jay Treaty with Great Britain, which angered France, now amid a revolution. The French had directed their navy to seize American merchant ships trading with Great Britain. When Pinckney arrived in France, the French informed him that no American minister would be recognized. This outraged Pinckney. The next year, President Adams appointed him as one of three commissioners, including Elbridge Gerry and John Marshall, to negotiate a treaty with the French. When the French, led by Foreign Minister Tallyrand, requested a bribe to facilitate negotiations, Pinckney angrily exploded, "No, no, not a sixpence!" He urged his government to raise "millions for defense but not one cent for tribute." He broke off discussions and then headed home without a deal, taking Marshall with him, leaving the more moderate Gerry behind. This event, known as the XYZ Affair after the related documents were published in 1798, strained the Adams presidency and led to the Quasi-War with France. Upon returning home, Pinckney accepted an appointment as a major general in the army, commanding all forces south of Maryland until the peace was finally negotiated in the summer of 1800.

In 1800, the Federalists, coordinated by Alexander Hamilton, selected Pinckney as their vice-presidential nominee, hoping he would help carry the South. However, the Adams-Pinckney ticket narrowly lost to Jefferson-Burr, 73 to 64. Hamilton had schemed to use the Electoral College results to supplant Adams with Pinckney, but Pinckney had declared he would accept no votes intended for Adams.

In 1804, Pinckney was put up as the Federalist candidate against the popular Thomas Jefferson. Neither party ran a campaign, and Jefferson won in a landslide, 162 to 14 electoral votes. Pinckney even lost South Carolina, making him the first major party candidate to lose his home state.

With Jefferson out of the picture in 1808, Pinckney ran again for president as a Federalist, this time against James Madison, a Democratic-Republican. A potential war was looming with France or Britain, and someone with military experience might appeal to the electorate. While the Federalists won Delaware and most of New England, Madison prevailed in a closer election, 122 to 47.

For the remainder of his life, Pinckney focused on his plantations and legal practice. He was the President-General of the Society of the Cincinnati from 1805 until his death. He was elected to the American Antiquarian Society in 1813.

Pinckney died on August 16, 1825, in his 79th year. He was buried at St. Michael's Churchyard in Charleston, South Carolina. His tombstone is engraved, "One of the founders of the American Republic. In war, he was a companion in arms and friend of Washington. In peace, he enjoyed his unchanging confidence."

Pinckney is honored in many ways:

- Castle Pinckney, a fort in Charleston Harbor.
- Pinckney Island National Wildlife Refuge, on the site of the Pinckney family's plantation.
- C. C. Pinckney Elementary school in Fort Jackson, South Carolina.
- Charles Pinckney Elementary School school in Mount Pleasant, South Carolina.
- Pinckney Elementary school in Lawrence, Kansas.
- SS *Charles C. Pinckney*, World War II, a 422-foot liberty ship built in Wilmington, North Carolina.

# SOUTH CAROLINA PATRIOTS

- Pinckney Street on Beacon Hill in Boston and in Madison, Wisconsin.
- Pinckneyville, Illinois, and Pinckney, Michigan.
- Pinckney Highway (SC 9) in Chester, South Carolina.
- In the television comedy series *The Epic Tales of Captain Underpants*, Charles Cotesworth Pinckney is often brought up as something of a running gag when one of the cast yells at a painting of him, "Darn you, Charles Cotesworth Pinckney!"

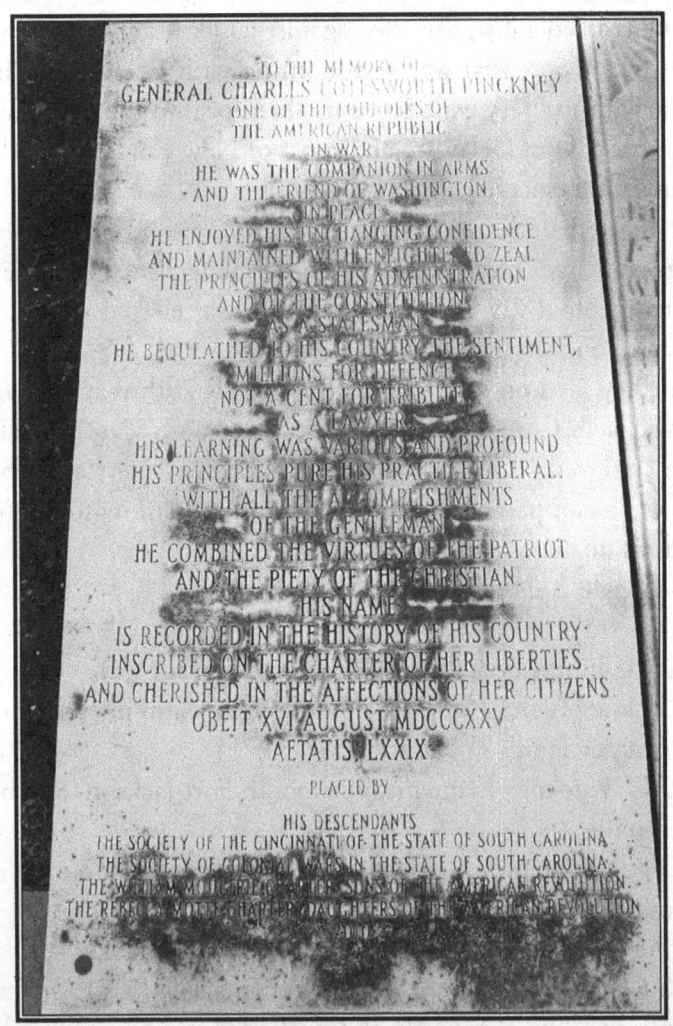

Charles Cotesworth Pinckney

# Edward Rutledge
## (1749–1800)

### Youngest to Sign the Declaration

Buried at Saint Philips Episcopal Church Cemetery, Charleston, South Carolina.

---

**Continental Congress • Signer of the Continental Association & Declaration of Independence • Military**

Edward Rutledge was a young lawyer from a privileged South Carolina family who, along with his brother John and his law partner, Charles Cotesworth Pinckney, became intimately involved in the independence movement. Rutledge signed the Continental Association and was the youngest to sign the Declaration of Independence. Later, he was the governor of South Carolina.

---

Rutledge was born in Charleston, Christ Church Parish, South Carolina, on November 23, 1749, the youngest of seven children of Dr. John Rutledge and his wife, Sarah (née Hart) Rutledge. The elder Rutledge was a physician of Scots-Irish roots. The mother was of English heritage.

Young Edward was educated by private tutors, including David Smith, who taught him seven languages. Rather than following in his father's footsteps to become a physician, like his older brothers John and Hugh, he studied law at the Middle Temple, one of the four Inns of Court in London. Rutledge was admitted to the English bar in 1772 and returned to Charleston to open a law practice.

Edward Rutledge

Rutledge was a noteworthy lawyer from the start. Soon after opening his practice in 1773, he won the release via grounds of *habeus corpus* of Thomas Powell, the newspaper publisher who had been imprisoned by the authorities for printing an article critical of the colonial government. The following year, Rutledge was named one of five delegates to the First Continental Congress from South Carolina.

On March 1, 1774, Rutledge married Henrietta Middleton, the daughter of fellow Continental Congressman Henry Middleton. The couple had three children: Henry, Edward, and Sarah. Later that year, on October 20, Rutledge and his brother John were among the five signers of the Continental Association from South Carolina, which also included his father-in-law, Henry Middleton, Christopher Gadsden, and Thomas Lynch, Sr. Though the junior member of the delegation at that time, with the retirements of Gadsden and Middleton from Congress and the debilitating stroke that hit Lynch, Edward Rutledge soon became the lead representative.

## Edward Rutledge (1749–1800)

Rutledge was an early proponent of a national constitution as the Congress debated independence. He was concerned the independent states would flounder without one. Thus, he initially resisted Richard Henry Lee's motion for independence in June 1776, believing the colonies were not ready. Though Rutledge had told John Adams he was in favor of independence when it came time to vote, South Carolina and Pennsylvania voted in the negative. Delaware was tied as a delegate was absent, and New York had no instructions and could not act. Rutledge, however, intimated he would change his vote to the majority should it be needed to pass the resolution. The next day, Delaware's delegates were all present and voted in the affirmative, providing a sufficient majority to declare independence. South Carolina then reversed its vote, adding to the majority. Edward Rutledge was then the youngest delegate to sign the Declaration of Independence.

Also, in June 1776, Rutledge was named to the Board of War for the colonies, overseeing the Continental Army. The Congress attempted to parley with the British, seeking to avoid further warfare. Benjamin Franklin had written a letter to Admiral Richard Howe, suggesting a meeting. Howe and his brother William had been named peace commissioners to seek a resolution from further hostilities. Known as the Staten Island Conference, the meeting was held on September 11, 1776, at the home of Colonel Christopher Billop on Staten Island. John Adams and Edward Rutledge served in the delegation with Franklin. The British had just captured New York City, and Howe felt he did not have the authority to negotiate such a resolution. Thus, the meeting ended in failure.

Rutledge left the Congress and returned home in November 1776. In 1778, he was elected to a seat in the South Carolina legislature. He also volunteered to serve in the South Carolina militia, in the Charleston Battalion of Artillery, attaining the rank of captain. When he was re-elected to the Continental Congress in 1779, he refused the seat on account of his military service. In February 1779, Rutledge participated in General William Moultrie's successful battle with the British at Port Royal Island, also known as the Battle of Beaufort.

The British invaded South Carolina in 1780, sacking Charleston in May. Rutledge and fellow co-signers of the Declaration of Independence,

Arthur Middleton and Thomas Heyward, were captured and imprisoned at St. Augustine, Florida. They were finally exchanged for other prisoners in July 1781.

Upon his release in 1782, Rutledge was returned to the South Carolina legislature, serving in 1782, 1786, 1788, and 1792 as the representative from Saint Philip and Saint Michael Parishes. He advocated for the taking of Loyalist property. Three times, he was named a presidential elector and aligned with the Federalists, though, in 1796, he voted for Southerners Jefferson and Pinkney.

In 1788, Rutledge attended the state's convention to ratify the US Constitution, voting in the affirmative. During this time, Rutledge also became a wealthy plantation owner.

Rutledge was nominated to be a justice on the US Supreme Court by George Washington in 1794, but he declined. Four years later, despite declining health, Rutledge was elected governor of South Carolina. Historian Robert T. Conrad wrote of Rutledge's appearance in 1846:

> The person of Mr. Rutledge was above the middle size, and inclining to corpulency; his complexion was florid and fair, and if not what would be termed a handsome man, the expression of his countenance was universally admired. He lost the greater part of his hair early in life, the remainder being perfectly white, and curling on his neck; so that had it not been for the goodness of his teeth, and the smoothness of his visage, and the fine flow of his spirits, he would have been considered a much older man than he was . . . Being latterly afflicted with gout, his gait was infirm, and he walked with a cane: before he was debilitated by this disease, his step was steady and quick, his arms usually folded across his breast, or his hands interlocked behind. His general demeanor was serene and composed, and when in a sitting posture, he usually rested his chin upon his hand, as if in serious contemplation.

As governor, Rutledge returned home to Charleston due to his gout. En route, on January 23, 1800, Rutledge suffered a stroke and died at age 50. Some contemporaries suggest the cause of death was apoplexy out of concern for George Washington's recent passing the prior month.

## Edward Rutledge (1749–1800)

Rutledge was laid to rest in Charleston at Saint Philip Episcopal Church. A stone at his tomb reads: "Beneath this Stone are Deposited the Remains of His Excellency Edward Rutledge Esq. Late Governor of this State, whom it pleased the almighty to take from this life Jany 23rd 1800 at the age of Fifty years."

The Edward Rutledge House in Charleston, since 1971, is a National Historic Landmark and is privately owned and operated as a bed and breakfast, the Governor's House Inn.

Edward Rutledge appears in Trumbull's paintings of the Declaration of Independence, standing on the far right.

Grave of Edward Rutledge

# John Rutledge
## (1739 – 1800)

### "The Dictator"

Buried at Saint Michaels Episcopal Church Cemetery, Charleston, South Carolina.

---

**Continental Congress • Signer of the Continental Association & US Constitution • US Supreme Court**

John Rutledge was a lawyer from a privileged South Carolina family who, along with his brother Edward, represented South Carolina in the Continental Congress. Rutledge signed the Continental Association and the US Constitution. He was also the first governor of newly independent South Carolina and later one of the first associate justices of the US Supreme Court. In 1795, he briefly became the second Chief Justice of the US Supreme Court.

---

Rutledge was born in Charleston, Christ Church Parish, South Carolina, on September 17, 1739. He was the oldest of seven children of Dr. John Rutledge and his wife, Sarah (née Hart) Rutledge. The elder Rutledge was a physician of Scots-Irish roots who had arrived with his brother, Andrew, in 1735. His mother was of English heritage and was only fifteen when he was born. Her father had dowered a large estate with the marriage, so the children were raised with great advantages.

Young John was educated by his father until his death in 1750. He was then tutored by an Anglican priest, Reverend Andrews. Next, John

## John Rutledge (1739–1800)

John Rutledge

was admitted to the Middle Temple, one of the four Inns of Court of the English judicial system in London, on October 11, 1754, at only fifteen. In 1756, Rutledge was an understudy with James Parsons, a local barrister in Charleston and his uncle, Andrew Rutledge, also an attorney. Upon finishing two years of study, Rutledge returned to England and was called to the English bar in 1760. He won several cases in the English courts before he returned to Charleston in 1761 to open his law practice. He also sought his first political office. He was first elected to the South Carolina Provincial Assembly in 1762, representing Christ-Church Parish in the Charleston area. He served until the start of the American Revolution.

On May 1, 1764, Rutledge married Elizabeth Grimké. Together, they had ten children, eight of whom lived to adulthood. Daughter Elizabeth later married Henry Laurens, Jr., the son of the President of the Continental Congress.

To reimburse the Crown for the cost of the French and Indian War, Parliament implemented the Stamp Act in March 1765. The stamps were to be affixed to various paper products throughout the Americas. This was met with strong resistance, including John Rutledge from South Carolina. He, Thomas Lynch, and Christopher Gadsden were appointed to meet in New York with other colonies in protest. This Stamp Act Congress penned a petition to Parliament. Rutledge, Edward Tilghman, and Philip Livingston were charged with the task. A portion of it read it was "the undoubted right of Englishmen, that no taxes be imposed on them but with their own consent, given personally, or by their representatives." The petition was unsuccessful, and chaos ensued throughout the colonies, including the destruction of stamps and persecution of Loyalists. In South Carolina, due to the absence of stamps, all legal proceedings came to a standstill. Ultimately, the act was repealed in 1766.

Rutledge continued his law practice during the intervening years and enriched himself via his plantations. By the early 1770s, tensions increased with Britain. When the Crown clamped down on Massachusetts following the Boston Tea Party in December 1773, many across the colonies rallied in sympathy. In July 1774, South Carolina met in Charleston and declared Henry Middleton, John Rutledge, Christopher Gadsden, Thomas Lynch, and Edward Rutledge would be delegates to the First Continental Congress to be held in Philadelphia in September. John, the elder Rutledge, was the chairman of the delegation.

At the Continental Congress, John Rutledge was very conservative, seeking reconciliation with Great Britain. Unlike his brother, he was against a move to independence at the time. It was at Rutledge's suggestion, after much debate on apportionment based on populations, that the colonies each simply received one vote. Ultimately, Congress passed the Continental Association, to which Rutledge and his brother were signers.

At the Second Continental Congress the following year, both Rutledges signed the Olive Branch Petition, seeking reconciliation with Great Britain. Rutledge urged the creation of new governments in the colonies based on constitutions, and in November 1775, returned to South Carolina to help draft the state's constitution, the first such document in the colonies. This was enacted in early 1776, and Rutledge was elected president (governor) of the state in March. He faced his first crisis in June when an attack by the British on Charleston. General Charles Lee had urged Moultrie's retreat from the unfinished fort on Sullivan Island, but Rutledge penned a short note, "General Lee wishes you to evacuate the fort. You will not without an order from me. I would sooner cut off my hand than write one." Moultrie was victorious, some say, thanks to the walls being made of palmetto trees and sand, which diminished the force of the cannonballs. Thus, the palmetto tree later became the state symbol.

Rutledge served as governor through his resignation in 1778 and then again from 1779 to 1782, earning the name "Dictator John" for his autocratic rule. In 1780, when the British captured Charleston, Rutledge escaped, functioning as a one-man government in exile until the Continental Army liberated the state. Following the victory at Cowpens and Nathanael Greene's taking of Charleston, John Mathewes then succeeded Rutledge as governor in 1782. Rutledge returned to the Continental Congress. In 1784, Rutledge was elected chief judge of the South Carolina Court of Chancery.

In 1787, Rutledge was a delegate to the Constitutional Convention in Philadelphia. He was a proponent of a strong chief executive and the limitations of the judiciary. He also was against landownership as a criterion for voting rights. During the deliberations, Rutledge was one of the primary authors of what became the Great Compromise, also known as the Connecticut Compromise, addressing how representation would be apportioned. It was agreed the Senate would have an equal number of representatives while the House would be based on population. Though the Southern delegates argued for fully counting slaves for the purpose of apportionment, it was agreed to reduce the ratio to three-fifths, thereby achieving political balance, North and South. It was also agreed that the international slave trade would not be prohibited before 1808. Additionally, the South Carolina delegates saw that the Fugitive Slave Clause was added to further protect slavery by requiring slaves to be returned to their states of labor. Rutledge signed the US Constitution and returned home to lead the effort of its adoption.

In the first presidential election, Rutledge received six electoral votes. Newly elected President George Washington appointed Rutledge as one of the four associate judges on the new US Supreme Court. Rutledge was unable to travel to the new capital in New York City, so he traveled a circuit, hearing local cases. After two years of this, on account of his health, Rutledge resigned. He had also been named South Carolina's Chief Justice of the Court of Common Pleas, which he accepted in March 1791. Another factor in his decision may have been the declining health of Elizabeth, his wife, who died in 1792. This loss deeply affected Rutledge, who is said to have fallen into depression and alcoholism and was beginning to suffer financial distress.

In 1795, when Chief Justice John Jay's resignation appeared imminent given his election as the governor of New York, Rutledge informed President Washington he would be willing to take the position. Washington agreed to the offer and asked the Senate to confirm Rutledge, not knowing of Rutledge's personal issues. Before leaving for Philadelphia, Rutledge denounced the recent Jay Treaty, preferring war with England over its adoption, and took his seat for the August term while the Senate was in recess.

While chief justice, two important cases were decided. In *United States v. Peters*, the Court ruled that federal district courts had no jurisdiction over crimes committed against Americans at sea. In *Talbot v. Janson*, the Court held that a citizen of the United States did not waive all claims to U.S. citizenship by either renouncing citizenship of an individual state or by becoming a citizen of another country. This set the precedent for the possibility of multiple citizenship.

Upon the Senate's return to session, many senators had difficulty with Rutledge's feelings about the Jay Treaty and were concerned about his mental and financial state that was being discussed in the newspapers. On December 15, 1795, the Senate voted 14 to 10 against Rutledge as Chief Justice. Disgraced, Rutledge first attempted suicide on December 26, 1795, by jumping off a wharf in Charleston Harbor. He was rescued by two slaves who saw him drowning. Rutledge then resigned on December 28, 1795, before his term would have lapsed. He left for home, the shortest-tenured Chief Justice in US history at only 138 days.

## John Rutledge (1739 – 1800)

He also resigned from the South Carolina Supreme Court citing health reasons. Rutledge did serve one more term in the South Carolina House of Representatives but was very frail in his retirement.

John Rutledge died in Charleston on July 18, 1800, at the age of 60. He was interred at St. Michael's Episcopal Church in Charleston.

Grave of John Rutledge

His grave inscription says, "On the 18th of July Anno Domini 1800 Departed this Life in the 61st Year of His Age. John Rutledge. Signer of the US Constitution." Said one Charleston newspaper:

> In the times that tried men's souls, and when the greatest abilities were requisite, Carolina looked to her John Rutledge, and confined her most important interests to his talents and virtues. Nor was she disappointed. What could be done by any man for his country, invaded, distressed, and over-run, was done for South-Carolina by this, her highly favored son. As a public speaker, he charmed and transported all who heard him: his eloquence would not suffer by a comparison with the most famous orators of antiquity.

One of Rutledge's houses has been renovated and is open to the public as the John Rutledge House Inn.

# Thomas Sumter
## (1734 – 1832)

### Carolina Gamecock

Buried at Thomas Sumter Memorial Park,
Sumter County, South Carolina.

**Military • Political**

Thomas Sumter, nicknamed the "Carolina Gamecock," was a brigadier general in the South Carolina militia during the American Revolution known by the enemy for his aggressive fighting style. He was initially a member of the Virginia militia and later a planter, politician, member of the US House of Representatives, and a US Senator. Fort Sumter in Charleston Harbor was named in his honor.

Thomas Sumter was born August 14, 1734, in Hanover County, Virginia, to William Sumter, a miller and former indentured servant, and his wife, Patience, a midwife. Sumter spent most of his early years assisting his father at the mill and tending livestock. He received only rudimentary schooling during these years.

As a young man, Sumter was a member of the Virginia militia and survived the ill-fated Braddock Expedition in 1755. During the French and Indian War, he rose to the rank of sergeant. From 1759 to 1761, Sumter participated in the Cherokee War. As that conflict with the natives ebbed, Sumter was selected for a diplomatic mission to the Cherokee nation known as the Timberlake Expedition led by Henry Timberlake

Thomas Sumter

and organized by Colonel Adam Stephen. They were accompanied by an interpreter named John McCormack and a servant. The goal was to renew friendship with the Overhill Cherokee towns.

During the expedition, while they were exploring a cave, their canoes drifted away on an icy stream. Sumter dove in and swam nearly a half-mile to retrieve them. The party was greeted warmly when they reached Tomotley on December 20, 1761. There a chief, Ostenaco ("Mankiller"), offered them a peace pipe. During the following weeks, peace ceremonies were held in surrounding Cherokee towns.

That spring, the party returned to Williamsburg, Virginia, with Ostenaco and several other tribal leaders. While there at the College of William and Mary, Ostenaco requested to meet with the King of England. Thomas Jefferson, who was a student at the time, later recalled Ostenaco:

I knew much of the great Outassete (Ostenaco), the warrior and orator of the Cherokee. He was always the guest of my father on his journeys to and from Williamsburg. I was in his camp when he made his great farewell oration to his people the evening before he departed for England. The moon was in full splendor, and to her, he seemed to address himself in his prayers for his own safety on the voyage and that of his people during his absence. His sounding voice, distinct articulation, animated action, and the solemn silence of his people at their several fires, filled me with awe and veneration, although I did not understand a single word he uttered.

A voyage commenced in May 1762 with Sumter and others accompanying the Indian delegation. In London, the natives were celebrities and received their audience with King George III. The Cherokee then accompanied Sumter back to the colonies, arriving in Charleston on August 25, 1762.

All was not well for Sumter at this point. He had petitioned Virginia for reimbursement of his travel expenses but was denied. This would seem to indicate Sumter's role in the voyage was not an official one. Without money and now in debt, Sumter was thrown into debtor's prison in Staunton, Virginia. Fortunately, a fellow soldier and friend, Joseph Martin, located him and requested to spend a night in jail with him. That evening, Martin handed Sumter some money and a tomahawk. Sumter then used the money to buy his way out of jail. Sumter then headed for South Carolina to start his life anew and escape any further difficulties with creditors.

Around 1764, Sumter settled in Stateburg, South Carolina, in Orangeburg County, along the Santee River. There, he became a merchant and opened a country store. He prospered and acquired property and slaves. In 1767, Sumter married Mary Cantey Jameson, a wealthy, crippled widow who was many years older than him. They moved in together on her plantation, Great Savannah, where they raised two children and became successful planters.

In 1775, as the Revolution began, Sumter was a member of the local Council of Safety and the provincial congress. He reentered military service as a captain. In December 1775, he participated in the "Snow Campaign" to subdue Loyalist forces. It was called this due to snowy weather.

In 1776, he raised a local militia group and was elevated to lieutenant colonel of the Second Regiment of the South Carolina Line. In June 1776, he served under General Charles Lee in the successful defense of Charleston at the Battle of Sullivan's Island.

From July to October 1776, Sumter was back fighting against the Cherokee with whom he had helped broker peace in the prior decade. He then fought the British in Georgia and St. Augustine from 1777 to 1778 before leaving the army at the rank of colonel on September 19, 1778. He returned to private life and was elected to the first South Carolina General Assembly following the new state constitution.

The British invaded South Carolina and captured Charleston in May 1780. They seemed poised to control the South and were on their way to victory. However, they made a fateful decision when Col. Banastre Tarleton's raiders burned down Sumter's plantation home. Sumter took this personally and immediately returned to the field and organized an army of local backcountry partisans who elected him their general. "Sumter's Brigade" spent the summer of 1780 as the only opposition to the British in South Carolina, engaging the enemy at Rocky Mount on July 30, Hanging Rock on August 6, and Fishing Creek on August 18. While they did not always win, the tough resistance raised the patriots' spirits until Nathanael Greene's army could join them. Sumter's brother William served as a captain during this time.

Recognizing Sumter's contributions, Governor Rutledge appointed him as a brigadier general in the South Carolina militia on October 6. Sumter's forces fought well at Fishdam Ford on November 9 and Blackstock's on November 20. The rebels routed Tarleton's force, losing only three killed and five wounded to nearly 200 casualties for the British. Unfortunately, Sumter was one of the severely wounded, taking a ball in the chest. He was out of commission for three months. After this battle, Tarleton commented that Sumter "fought like a gamecock," and Cornwallis described the Gamecock as his "greatest plague."

While Sumter was convalescing, Washington sent Nathanael Greene to lead the Southern Department, overlooking Sumter. Back in the

## Thomas Sumter (1734–1832)

saddle in February 1781, Sumter led troops at Fort Gransby but did not appreciate the commands he was receiving from on high in the army of Nathanael Greene. Sumter attempted to resign, but Greene did not permit it. Sumter then fought at Orangeburg in May.

In July, Sumter then joined with Greene and led "the raid of the dog days" into the low country of South Carolina, riding with Francis Marion. However, he could not reconcile his differences with leadership, and his resignation was accepted in February 1782, ending his military career.

Sumter remained involved in politics. He served eight terms in the General Assembly of South Carolina between 1776 and 1790. In 1783 he helped to found the town of Stateburg, South Carolina. He promoted it as the site of the new state capital, but this was not to be. After the passage of the new US Constitution, Sumter was a member of the First Congress, serving in the US House of Representatives from 1789 to 1793. During this time, in 1792, Sumter was reunited with his old friend, Joseph Martin, and repaid him the money that had helped him get out of debtors' prison thirty years earlier.

Sumter was reelected to the House of Representatives and served from 1797 to 1801. After being selected by the South Carolina legislature, he jumped to the Senate to replace Charles Pinckney, who had resigned. He served as a US Senator for ten years until December 16, 1810. While in the Congress, Sumter was a Democratic-Republican, backing the Jeffersonians who were friendlier to the backcountry farmers.

Now retired from the Senate in his mid-70s, Sumter watched his son, Thomas Sumter Jr., serve as the United States Ambassador to the Portuguese Court while exiled in Brazil, at Rio de Janeiro 1810 to 1819. Thomas Jr. had married Natalie De Lage de Volude, the daughter of French nobility, sent by her parents to America for her safety during the French Revolution. She was raised in New York City from 1794 to 1801 by Vice President Aaron Burr as his ward, alongside his daughter Theodosia.

Thomas Sumter lived to the age of 97, the last surviving general from the American Revolution. On June 1, 1832, he died at South Mount, his plantation near Stateburg, South Carolina. He was buried at what is now the Thomas Sumter Memorial Park in Sumter County, South Carolina.

Colonel Thomas De Lage Sumter, a grandson of Thomas Sumter, served in the US Army during the Second Seminole War (1835-1842). He later represented South Carolina in the United States House of Representatives.

Thomas Sumter's crypt.

## Thomas Sumter (1734–1832)

Fort Sumter, planned after the War of 1812, was erected in Charleston Harbor and named after him. His name would then become forever associated with the opening volleys of the Civil War in 1861.

The town of Sumter, South Carolina, was named after him. They erected a memorial to him, and the town has been dubbed "The Gamecock City."

Four states have counties named after him: Alabama, Florida, Georgia, and South Carolina.

Since 1903, the University of South Carolina's nickname has been "The Fighting Gamecocks."

At the state capitol in Columbia, South Carolina, Sumter shares a monument, erected in 1913, with Francis Marion and Andrew Pickens.

# Sources

**Books, Magazines, Journals, Files:**

Alexander, Edward P. *Revolutionary Conservative: James Duane of New York*. New York: Ams Press, 1978.

Anthony, Katharine Susan. *First Lady of the Revolution; The Life of Mercy Otis Warren*. Port Washington, N.Y.: Kennikat Press, 1972.

Appleby, Joyce. *Inheriting the Revolution: The First Generation of Americans*. Cambridge, Massachusetts: Harvard University Press, 2000.

Atkinson, Rick. *The British Are Coming: The War for America, Lexington to Princeton, 1775–1777*. New York: Henry Holt & Co. 2019.

Bordewich, Fergus M. *The First Congress: How James Madison, George Washington, and a Group of Extraordinary Men Invented the Government*. New York: Simon and Schuster Paperbacks, 2016.

Boudreau, George W. *Independence: A Guide to Historic Philadelphia*. Yardley, Pennsylvania: Westholme Publishing, LLC. 2012.

Bowen, Catherine Drinker. *Miracle at Philadelphia: The Story of the Constitutional Convention May to September 1787*. Boston, Massachusetts: Little, Brown & Company, 1966.

Breen, T.H, *George Washington's Journey: The President Forges a New Nation*. New York: Simon & Schuster. 2016.

Brookhiser, Richard. *Gentleman Revolutionary: Gouverneur Morris The Rake Who Wrote the Constitution*. New York: Free Press, 2003.

———. *John Marshall: The Man Who Made the Supreme Court*. New York: Basic Books. 2018.

Brush, Edward Hale. *Rufus King and His Times*. New York: N.L. Brown, 1926.

Chadwick, Bruce. *I Am Murdered: George Wythe, Thomas Jefferson, and the Killing That Shocked a New Nation*. Hoboken, New Jersey: John Wiley & Sons, 2009.

Chambers, II, John Whiteclay. *The Oxford Companion to American Military History*. Oxford: Oxford University Press, 1999.

Commager, Henry Steele & Richard B. Morris. *The Spirit of 'Seventy-Six: The Story of the American Revolution as Told by Participants*. New York: Harper & Rowe, 1967.

Cole, Ryan. *Light-Horse Harry Lee: The Rise and Fall of a Revolutionary Hero*. Washington, D.C.: Regnery History. 2019.

Conlin, Joseph R. *The Morrow Book of Quotations in American History*. New York: William Morrow and Company, Inc., 1984.

Daniels, Jonathan. *Ordeal of Ambition*. Garden City, New York: Doubleday & Company, Inc., 1970.

Dann, John C. *The Revolution Remembered: Eyewitness Accounts of the War for Independence*. Chicago: University of Chicago Press, 1980.

# SOURCES

DeRose, Chris. *Founding Rivals: Madison vs. Monroe: The Bill of Rights and the Election that Saved a Nation.* New York: MJF Books, 2011.

Drury, Bob & Tom Clavin. *Valley Forge.* New York: Simon & Schuster. 2018.

Ellis, Joseph J. *Revolutionary Summer: The Birth of American Independence.* New York: Alfred A. Knopf, 2013.

———. *The Quartet: Orchestrating the Second American Revolution, 1783–1789.* New York: Alfred A. Knopf, 2015.

———. *His Excellency: George Washington.* New York: Alfred A. Knopf, 2004.

Flexner, James Thomas. *George Washington in the American Revolution, 1775–1783.* Boston: Little, Brown & Company, 1967.

Flower, Lenore Embick. "Visit of President George Washington to Carlisle, 1794." Carlisle, Pennsylvania: The Hamilton Library and Cumberland County Historical Society, 1932.

Gerlach, Don R. *Proud Patriot: Philip Schuyler and the War of Independence, 1775–1783.* Syracuse, N.Y.: Syracuse University Press, 1987.

Goodrich, Charles A. *Lives of the Signers of the Declaration of Independence.* Charlotteville, N.Y.: SamHar Press, 1976.

Griffith, IV, William R. *The Battle of Lake George: England's First Triumph in the French and Indian War.* Charleston, South Carolina: The History Press, 2016.

Grossman, Mark. *Encyclopedia of the Continental Congress.* Armenia, New York: Grey House Publishing, 2015.

Hamilton, Edward P. *Fort Ticonderoga: Key to a Continent.* Boston: Little, Brown & Company, 1964.

Isenberg, Nancy. *Fallen Founder: The Life of Aaron Burr.* New York: Penguin Group, 2007.

Kennedy, Roger G. *Burr, Hamilton, and Jefferson: A Study in Character.* New York: Oxford University Press, 1999.

Kiernan, Denise & Joseph D'Agnese. *Signing Their Lives Away: The Fame and Misfortune of the Men Who Signed the Declaration of Independence.* Philadelphia: Quirk Books, 2008.

———. *Signing Their Rights Away: The Fame and Misfortune of the Men Who Signed the United States Constitution.* Philadelphia: Quirk Books, 2011.

Klarman, Michael J. *The Framers' Coup: The Making of the United States Constitution.* New York: Oxford University Press, 2016.

Langguth, A. J. *Patriots.* New York: Simon and Schuster, 1988.

Larson, Edward J. *A Magnificent Catastrophe.* New York: Free Press, 2007.

Lee, Mike. Written *Out of History: The Forgotten Founders Who Fought Big Government.* New York: Penguin Books, 2017.

Lewis, James E., Jr., *The Burr Conspiracy: Uncovering the Story of an Early American Crisis,* Princeton: Princeton University Press, 2017.

Lockridge, Ross Franklin. *The Harrisons.* 1941.

Lomask, Milton. *Aaron Burr: The Years from Princeton to Vice President, 1756–1805.* New York: Farrar Straus Giroux, 1979.

Lossing, Benson J. *Pictorial Field Book of the Revolution.* New York: Harper Brothers. 1851.

Maier, Pauline. *American Scripture: Making the Declaration of Independence*. New York: Alfred A. Knopf, Inc., 1997.
McCullough, David. *John Adams*. New York: Simon & Schuster, 2002.
Meltzer, Brad & Josh Mensch. *The First Conspiracy: The Secret Plot to Kill George Washington*. New York: Flat Iron Books. 2018.
Middlekauff, Robert. *The Glorious Cause: The American Revolution, 1763–1789*. Oxford: Oxford University Press, 2005.
Miller, Jr., Arthur P. & Marjorie L. Miller. *Pennsylvania Battlefields and Military Landmarks*. Mechanicsburg, Pennsylvania: Stackpole Books, 2000.
Millett, Allan R. & Peter Maslowski. *For the Common Defense: A Military History of the United States of America*. New York: The Free Press, 1984.
Moore, Charles. *The Family Life of George Washington*. New York: Houghton Mifflin, 1926.
Nagel, Paul C. *The Lees of Virginia: Seven Generations of an American Family*. Oxford: Oxford University Press, 1990.
O'Connell, Robert L. *Revolutionary: George Washington at War*. New York: Random House. 2019.
Racove, Jack N. *Revolutionaries: A New History of the Invention of America*. New York: Houghton Mifflin Harcourt, 2011.
Raphael, Ray. *Founding Myths: Stories That Hide Our Patriotic Past*. New York: MJF Books, 2004.
Rossiter, Clinton. *1787 The Grand Convention*. New York: The Macmillan Company, 1966.
Seymour, Joseph. *The Pennsylvania Associators, 1747–1777*. Yardley, Pennsylvania: Westholme Publishing, LLC. 2012.
Schweikart, Larry & Michael Allen. *A Patriot's History of the United States from Columbus's Great Discovery to the War on Terror*. New York: Penguin, 2004.
Sharp, Arthur G. *Not Your Father's Founders*. Avon, Massachusetts: Adams Media, 2012.
Stahr, Walter. *John Jay: Founding Father*. New York: Diversion Books, 2017.
Taafee, Stephen R. *The Philadelphia Campaign, 1777–1778*. Lawrence, Kansas: University of Kansas Press, 2003.
Tinkcom, Harry Marlin, *The Republicans and the Federalists in Pennsylvania, 1790–1801*. Harrisburg, Pennsylvania: Pennsylvania Historical and Museum Commission. 1950.
Ward, Matthew C. *Breaking the Backcountry: The Seven Years' War in Virginia and Pennsylvania, 1754–1765*. Pittsburgh, Pennsylvania: University of Pittsburgh Press, 2003.
Weisberger, Bernard A. *America Afire: Jefferson, Adams, and the Revolutionary Election of 1800*. New York: HarperCollins, 2000.
Wood, Gordon S. *The Radicalism of the American Revolution*. New York: Vintage Books, 1993.
———. *Empire of Liberty: A History of the Early Republic, 1789–1815*. New York: Penguin Books, 2004.
———. *Revolutionary Characters: What Made the Founders Different*. New York: Penguin Books, 2006.

# SOURCES

———. *The Americanization of Benjamin Franklin*. Oxford: Oxford University Press, 2009.

Wright, Benjamin F. *The Federalist: The Famous Papers on the Principles of American Government: Alexander Hamilton, James Madison, John Jay*. New York: Metro Books, 2002.

Zobel, Hiller B. *The Boston Massacre*. New York: W. W. Norton & Company, 1970.

**Video Resources:**

Guelzo, Allen C. The Great Courses: *America's Founding Fathers* (Course N. 8525). Chantilly, Virginia: The Teaching Company, 2017.

**Online Resources:**

Archives.gov – for information on the Constitutional Convention.
CauseofLiberty.blogspot.com – for information on Daniel Carroll.
ColonialHall.com – for information about the signers of the Declaration of Independence.
DSDI1776.com – for information on many Founders.
FamousAmericans.net – for information on many Founders.
FindaGrave.com – for burial information, vital statistics and obituaries.
FirstLadies.org – for information on Abigail Adams.
Newspapers.com – Hundreds of newspaper articles were accessed—too numerous to mention here.
NPS.gov – for information on various park sites.
TeachingAmericanHistory.com – for information on Charles Pinckney and George Wythe.
TheHistoryJunkie.com – for information on multiple Founders.
USHistory.org – for information on multiple Founders.
Wikipedia.com – for general historical information.

# Index

Adams, John, 12, 19, 22, 56, 78–79, 83
Adams, Samuel, vi, 17, 19, 31, 56
Articles of Confederation, vi, 1, 3, 23, 25–26, 29, 31, 33, 43, 45–46, 71
Boston, Massachusetts, v, 20, 80, 88
Camden, Battle of, v–vi, 10, 13, 15–16, 36–37, 39–40
Charleston, South Carolina, v–vi, 1–2, 9–10, 15, 17–26, 29, 31–37, 39–41, 43, 46–48, 50–52, 54, 57, 59, 61, 63, 66, 69–70, 72–76, 78–79, 81, 83–93, 95–96, 99
Constitution, US, 5, 8–11, 22, 29, 31–32, 63, 69, 71–72, 74, 77–78, 83–84, 86, 88–89, 92, 97
Continental Association, 17, 20, 54, 81–82, 86, 88
Cowpens, Battle of, v–vi, 22, 66, 68, 89
Davie, William Richardson, vi, 8–12
Declaration of Independence, vi, 23–24, 26–27, 48, 50, 53–54, 56, 75, 81, 83, 85
De Kalb, Baron Johan Robais, vi, 13–16
France, vi, 8, 12, 15, 74–75, 78–79
Franklin, Benjamin, 15, 56, 83
Gadsden, Christopher, vi, 17–22, 30–32, 45–46, 51, 55, 82, 88
Heyward, Thomas Jr., vi, 19, 23–28, 31, 44–45, 50, 84
Hutson, Richard, vi, 29–33, 45–46
Jefferson, Thomas, 73–74, 79, 84, 94
Laurens, Henry, v–vi, 1–7, 20, 31, 45–46
Madison, James, 9, 12, 71, 74, 79
Marion, Francis, vi, 34–42, 66, 97, 99
Mathews, John Mathews, vi, 22, 24, 41, 43–47
Middleton, Arthur, 31, 46, 48–54, 75, 84
Middleton, Henry, 19, 45, 48, 54–58, 75, 82, 88
Moultrie, William, vi, 22, 25, 36, 59–63, 76, 89
New York, New York, v, 1, 15, 19, 31, 36, 83, 88, 90, 97
Philadelphia, Pennsylvania, v, 3, 7, 10, 18, 20, 25, 31, 45–46, 56, 71, 72, 76–77, 88–90
Pickens, Andrew, vi, 37, 41, 64–68, 99
Pinckney, Charles, vi, 43, 69–74, 97
Pinckney, Charles Cotesworth, vi, 74–81
Rutledge, Edward, vi, 19, 47, 50–51, 56, 63, 81–86, 88
Rutledge, John, vi, 19, 21, 39, 45–46, 55, 67, 81–82, 86–92, 96
Sumter, Thomas, vi, 37–40, 66, 93–99
Washington, George, 15–16, 20, 22, 71, 76, 78–79, 84, 90–96
XYZ Affair, 74, 78
York, Pennsylvania, v, 3, 7, 25, 31, 45

www.ingramcontent.com/pod-product-compliance
Lightning Source LLC
Chambersburg PA
CBHW011256040426
42453CB00015B/2426